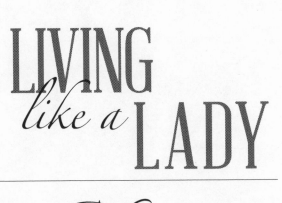

LIVING
like a LADY

---

*W*hen you have
CANCER

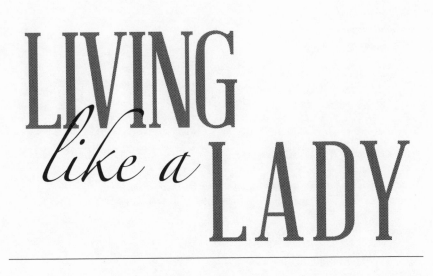

LIVING
like a LADY

When you have
CANCER

DONNA A. HECKLER

authorHOUSE®

AuthorHouse™ LLC
1663 Liberty Drive
Bloomington, IN 47403
www.authorhouse.com
Phone: 1-800-839-8640

Published by AuthorHouse 08/28/2014

ISBN: 978-1-4969-2898-6 (sc)
ISBN: 978-1-4969-2899-3 (hc)
ISBN: 978-1-4969-2893-1 (e)

Library of Congress Control Number: 2014913304

DEDICATION

I dedicate this book to the angels in my life.

To those whose halos are so shiny from the
smiles they share and the good they do.

To those who never realized how a simple, kind word made my day.

To those who cleaned my cat's litter box or my
closet, because it was what was needed.

To those who traveled the many miles to visit
and those who lived next door.

To those whom I met in an instant and will think about forever.

To those whom I am blessed to call my family and my dear friends.

To my family - Al, Gerry, Karen, Jennifer, Andy,
Nick, Leah, Fiona, Audrey, Steve, Troy,

Angela, Ann, Bill, Brian, Bryan, Bruce, Carol, Cathy, Chelsey, Chris,
Deborah, Doni, Ed, Elizabeth, Fran, Gary, George, Jackie, Jana, Jane,
Jen, Jenni, Jerry, Jimmy, Johanna, John, Joyce, Juan, Karen, Kathy,
Kathy, Kevin, Kristina, Laura, Leo, Leon, Linda, Lisa, Liz, Lou,
Mark, Maureen, Maureen, MaryBeth, Miranda, Patty, Paula, Perri,
Richard, Sally, Scott, Shane, Sherri, Steph, Suzie, Tom, Tony, Ward.

TABLE OF CONTENTS

You have cancer. Now what? A team of specialists will treat the disease, but what about you, the radiant lady inside? This book is that guide, to use as you need, to address the ladylike issues you may face as you go through treatment. Each section offers information on topics about which ladies need to know, but are often not told.

YOUR RADIANT SELF

- Why does hair fall out?
- Can the loss of hair be prevented or reversed?
- How should you manage the process of losing your hair?
- What do you do with that new bald head? How do you protect it?
- What is the impact of your loss of hair on others?
- Where do you lose your hair? Just on your head?

- The importance of water
- How to hydrate your skin
- Be gentle
- Body parts that get dry – that you never considered before

- Types of reconstructive surgery to consider and their phases
- Just in case, the complications

FASHION, FOOD, FATIGUE

- Clothing consideration for port access
- Clothing considerations for your surgery, especially mastectomy or double mastectomy
- What to wear when you have expanders, and they are expanding
- Being comfortable when you go through radiation
- Yes, a bathing suit

- If you have no appetite, what to eat
- How to stimulate your appetite
- The role of supplements
- The role of peppermint
- Plastic utensils

- The role of exercise
- To nap or not to nap
- Finally a good excuse to...watch a movie during the day, etc. etc.
- Might a "spa" day help?

FABULOUS FUTURE

Foreword

According to the American Cancer Society this year over 810,000 women in the United States will be diagnosed with cancer. Of these, over 232,000 will be diagnosed with breast cancer — 29% of all new cases. The majority of these women will undergo surgery, and many will experience chemotherapy and radiation with their attendant side effects.

In this book, Donna Heckler tells us of her own journey through diagnosis, chemotherapy, surgery, and radiation. Her use of journaling during her experience (reproduced in sidebars) allows us to accompany her during her ups and downs as if first hand. Her story serves not just to document her odyssey from diagnosis to survivorship, but imparts myriad pieces of advice for others going through the same or similar treatment.

From make-up tips to sunscreen on a bald pate to how to deal with hot flashes, Donna shares her wealth of knowledge. A resilient lady, a corporate executive, Donna's humor, will, spirit, and sustaining faith helped her along her road to wellness. Because of her experience she is able to help others, and teach them those tricks she learned along the way (such as plastic versus metal utensils and taste).

My hope is that all who read this are able to be radiant ladies, allowing the inner spirit to shine through. As Donna's dad pointed out to her, be like a butterfly emerging from a cocoon.

Diane M. Radford MD, FACS, FRCSEd
Breast Surgical Oncologist
St. Louis, MO
August 2014

INTRODUCTION

By way of introduction, I am Donna. I often start notes or emails to people this way, so why not a book? I am your storyteller, narrator, fact finder, and author. At least, that is what I am now.

It wasn't always like that. I used to be a "high-powered" executive. The corporate "girl." The woman around town who knew every restaurant and every chef, who would never miss a gala if she could help it. And then, I got cancer.

Perhaps I should start by telling you my story. As someone reading this who has cancer or has a friend or family member with cancer, you know there is always a story. As well there should be. Something like cancer touches us, influences us, shapes us, thus the story is important.

For me, the story probably starts when I fell and injured my leg. Really, you may ask? Yes, really. You see, I was stepping out of an elevator in a motel and slipped. In a freak accident, my leg twisted and was severely damaged. There was concern that I might not walk again, and that panicked me. I have heard many things about cancer, one of which is that every body has cells that have the potential to be cancerous – that it can be a stressful situation that unleashes the cancer. I don't know if this is true or not. What I do know is that I was in a wheelchair for six months and had only been walking without crutches for two months when I discovered my breast cancer. My OB-GYN thought the cancer had developed over about eight months. And, in that time it grew to 10cm and Stage 3, a very aggressive and fast growing cancer. Given the speed with which it developed, apparently I had the propensity and more than one unhappy, panicked cell in my body.

The company I was with had been struggling, and knowing this, I had been out interviewing for a new opportunity. Talk about a day of highs and lows. I had a great interview and several hours later learned I had breast cancer. And so, the question became do I stay home and focus on fighting the cancer? Or, do I go out, work at a job with considerable travel, and live my life? I chose to work. I chose to live my life. I tried to live like a lady every step of the way.

From the beginning, I knew there were a number of things I *didn't* want to do. I did not want to spell cancer with a capital C – it didn't deserve that. I didn't want to give in to it. I wasn't sure about the whole "fight" thing. Yes, I wanted to fight off the disease. But, for me, that was the medical part. I didn't want to change my life for cancer. I wanted to LIVE my life while my doctors and I took on the disease.

But, that is where things got tricky. I had no shortage of medical information available to me, and we are so fortunate with the strides that have been made in treating cancer. Beyond this, however, I wanted more. I wanted to know how to LIVE as I went through this. And, more to the point, Live Like A Lady, despite everything happening to my body.

I just couldn't find the material I was seeking. I met women who had various forms of cancer, and they each shared morsels they had gleaned that ultimately would help me with my journey. But, wasn't there a compendium of knowledge? Why did I and these other women have to discover these things on our own? What things? Well, things like that chemo may cause not just the hair on your head to fall out, but your nose hair, eyebrows, eyelashes, your hair "down there" to disappear. So unladylike. But, if you know these things might happen, at least you can prepare yourself for them. And, if they do happen to you, there are tricks and tips that will help you look and feel like the lady you are.

For me, I took that job. I put on make-up, threw on my wig, and went to work as an executive everyday for a new company, and no one was the wiser. The more I explored this new cancer journey, the more I discovered other women who had done the same thing. They had lived their life while they had cancer.

Whether I accomplished it or not, I did try to be my radiant self each and every day as I went through cancer. True, some days I was more radiant that others. But, that didn't mean that I didn't embrace what was possible for that day. Being radiant for the day, for me, started with my spirit and my faith. I found my faith and spirit getting stronger as I physically got weaker. Faith and spirit allowed me to start the day with a smile. But, to be prepared for work every day, I needed more than a smile. So, along the way, I learned what I could do to help me live radiantly. Radiantly for me means allowing your inner spirit to shine through, and doing what you can to support and work with your body's physical changes. We should not, each of us, have to start from scratch each time. My hope is that this book will provide the next woman going through cancer with an understanding of what might occur as well as some practical tips, tricks, and insights into living through the disease.

Are you going to hear more of my journey through this book? Yes, it is my story. But, it is not just mine. I have spoken with and interviewed women who have gone through various cancers and included their thoughts and insights as well. Doctors who are specialists have also contributed to this book, reading the chapters, discussing their areas of expertise, and providing insights. Experts in other fields are also included. For example, Saks Fifth Avenue has always strongly supported cancer efforts. One of their make-up artists, who routinely goes to chemo facilities to do the make-up of patients, contributed application tips that may help you feel more radiant.

Many wonderful medical books are available that focus on the "fight", the "battle" you will undergo. And, you will do that! I wanted this book to be about living, how to carry on with life while fighting. The overall focus is not on breast cancer, though there are a few chapters specific to that. I hope to talk to all ladies going through a cancer journey. The first chapter talks about the fact that you will lose your hair, especially if you require chemo. The book ends with the chapter that your hair will grow back. In between are chapters about everything from make-up choice to how dry your skin will be to what "girlfriends" might want to do to help to what clothes to wear as you go through radiation, and more.

The book is designed so that you don't have to read it straight through. Of course, you can if you would like, but, knowing that different things bother us on different days, you can also read about what matters to you on a particular day. By the way, be prepared to laugh. You might also cry. Both are ok. And yes, some people have said that they laugh and cry at the same time as they read through the stories shared here. During my cancer journey, I kept a blog on the private Caring Bridge site, capturing the humorous, meaningful, and just plain exhausting events along the way. In sidebars throughout the book, I include pieces from my blog entries as well as stories and insights from other ladies who have dealt with cancer.

What I know for certain is that there are probably things I have missed in writing this book. No matter how many ladies with cancer I speak with, no matter how many doctors or other experts, the fact remains that each of our journeys is unique, and no one book can address every potential concern or represent all experiences.

My hope is that, ultimately, each of you reading this walks away with one insight or one thought or one idea that might make you or your loved one going through cancer feel like she can LIVE LIKE A LADY.

YOUR RADIANT SELF

101 THINGS TO DO WHEN YOUR HAIR FALLS OUT

An early question every patient asks her oncologist when she discovers she has cancer is "Will my hair fall out?" Most likely, yes! We know, not the word you were hoping to hear. But, it does happen, especially from your chemo treatments, and you will be ok.

So, let's explore this hair situation right from the start. Your hair will most likely begin to fall out after your first chemo treatment. As you will often hear throughout this book, chemo is exceptionally good at killing fast growing cells such as cancer. However, it kills all fast growing cells, including your hair follicles, where rapidly dividing cells reside.

Part of what is so dispiriting in the cancer battle is the lack of control. Your hair, one piece of you that you have always been able to "do something with," is now doing its own thing. And, you can't stop it. However, you do have options.

CUTTING IT

If you have longer hair, you may consider cutting it a bit shorter before you start your chemo. One advantage of this is that you become accustomed to yourself with shorter hair. You ease into

> **Donna**
>
> *I am saving the biggest news of all for last - we cut my hair last night....SHORT! I lost a little already yesterday morning and had an appointment with my dear friends Kevin and Bill already for a little trim. But, when we started messing with it, we decided that we should take it rather short right from the beginning.*
>
> *I haven't had short hair since I was about 7 or 8. We were at a little festival and I wanted to toss ping pong balls into a goldfish bowl, and the woman said, "Can I help you, son?" I will never forget that - and I have never had short hair since. So, this was THE traumatic event for me so far.*
>
> *All that being said, it is sorta cute!! If I am brave enough, I will put a picture up on my blog with this short hair.*

the process of losing your hair in this way. Others may prefer to keep it long just as long as they can.

Ultimately, the choice is yours, but, keep in mind that there are many things that you will be losing control of, so controlling that hair of yours by cutting it may help you feel like you have some ability to direct the events around you.

LETTING IT FALL OUT NATURALLY

How will you know if your hair is falling out? If you are like most women, you will begin to pull on it as soon as you leave your first chemo. How quickly do these drugs take effect after all? Most likely, it won't fall out on day one of chemo or even day two or three. You need to give it a few days. However, it is not uncommon to start to see strands falling out by day five or so. Of course,

> ### Donna
>
> *So I have to share a little story from this morning... hopefully it will cause a chuckle to start your day!*
>
> *I stumbled out of bed and headed for my coffee. Halfway through the kitchen a cricket jumped on my foot. I jumped a mile and let out a scream. Now, many of you know that I have two cats - Honey and Muffin. Their sole job in this house is disposing of crickets, spiders and the occasional mouse. They typically fail miserably at this job - as they seem to think these are toys for them!*
>
> *So, when this cricket jumped, my natural inclination was to call for my two monster cats to take care of this problem. Of course they looked at it and looked at me with a "but we don't feel like playing now" look.*
>
> *As I looked at the cricket, I realized he wasn't moving. Hmmmm... usually they hop away when a cat comes near. I looked closer, and sure enough, the cricket's legs (feet, paws??? my vet brother-in-law will have to explain this part to me) were tangled up in a long strand of blond hair!!!*
>
> *Apparently, as I jumped a bit more hair fell out - and that, in fact, was the undoing of this poor cricket. Death by hair tangling!! I think I need to write a book - 101 Things To Do With Your Hair As It Falls Out!!*
>
> *I hope you are now starting your day with a smile!*

like everything else on this journey, it can be different for everyone, depending upon your hair, your body, your treatments.

Where to look for the strands of hair? Your comb and hairbrush are obvious, but many women start to realize their hair is coming out when they see some on the pillow in the morning. Good morning, you have lost hair isn't the best way to get your day started, but it is something you may have to get used to.

The first several weeks you will experience strands of hair falling out. As you move into week three, it may come out as several strands at a time or even clumps. When this happened to me, I could hardly keep my hands away from my head. Really, I kept asking myself, is it really coming out? The answer was yes, and each time I reached up, I pulled a little bit more out.

By the end of the third week of treatment, my hair was falling out in great clumps. A question that many women ask when going through chemo is, is there a way to prevent the hair from falling out?

The blogs will tell you of something called a penguin cap that basically freezes your head, in an effort to prevent the hair from falling out. A few concerns are worth mentioning with the cap. 1. Your hair will fall out anyway. 2. The cap is very uncomfortable. 3. The point of chemo is to kill the cancer throughout your body. If by freezing you are preventing the chemo from getting to your head and hair, then you are preventing the chemo from working on any little cancer cells that might be in your brain.

Like most women, at the outset, I was hopeful that this cap might work. I checked around. It was in speaking with my chemo nurses that I realized that a few months without hair was far better than a metastasis to the brain.

My father, an engineer and man of science, who wasn't quite sure how to handle his daughter having breast cancer, did offer up some sage advice assuring

> **Donna**
> *Happy Sunday...*
>
> *I am feeling great still. But.....I lost huge handfuls of hair yesterday. I don't like this one bit. I know that is superficial and that hair will grow back. But still......not loving this side effect at all.*

me, "Honey, if you are losing your hair, it means your treatment is working." So many times I had to turn to that phrase and remind myself that loss of hair is a visual indication that the chemo is working.

To Shave Or Not To Shave

My cancer treatment started with chemo. So, from the very beginning, I started thinking about getting my hair shaved off. That becomes another opportunity to take control. Many people, from friends to my hairdressers, advised me to shave it off, several suggesting that we turn it into a party, with some girlfriends and a glass of wine in hand.

I finally got to a point where I wanted it off. I wanted this part to be finished, I was so sick of seeing it fall out. Emotionally, I had been preparing to do this, but even though some women choose to do so, I couldn't begin to think about doing it as a party. I wasn't sure how I would react, so I wanted it to be more private.

While I had been thinking about having the remainder of my hair shaved off, the ultimate decision to do it was rather spontaneous.

LIFE WITH NO HAIR

Once you have lost your hair, you have new considerations. You lose much of your body heat through your head. So, without hair, you may get rather chilly. Thus, the scarves, hats, and wigs are not just a fashion statement, but also keep you warm. Another consideration, don't forget sunscreen. That head of yours hasn't seen this much light in a long time. Last thing you need is to get sunburned on top of your head through all of this!

Donna

Let your hair hang out — but only if you can. I, in fact, cannot anymore. I got it shaved today. Here's the story. I wanted to take a shower, but so much hair kept falling out that I thought I should try to pull as much out as possible before the shower. Took a shower, washed what little I had left, and even more came out.

Afterwards, Mom and I went to do some errands, meet with a nutritionist, go out to lunch, get my next Neulasta shot, and stop at a wig store. While I had already purchased one wig, we wanted to get a "halo" (Here's hoping God already has one polished up for me). These fit around the head, allowing hair to peek out from under your hat.

In the course of this, we found another wig – very cute. We were talking with the saleswoman about how much hair was coming out, and she said that they have a salon there where they shave the heads and did we just want to get it over and done with? I jumped at the idea – as I have been dealing with the mess for a week or so now. Mom, on the other hand, wasn't so sure.

They took us to the back room, got me settled, and put the shaver in Mom's hand suggesting that she do the first swipe. She did that well, but after the second and third, she had to catch her breath a bit, outside. I was not watching, so I had no idea what she was seeing.

But, it is done! We are both troopers in this one! Honestly, by the time I got to this place, I was really ready for it. It is horrible seeing bits of hair fall out. Besides which, it can't possibly be sanitary. Lest I forget, I feel great, evident by all our activities today!

For anyone ready to have a toast tonight, here's to the continuing journey and the many experiences we have along the way.

Beyond the practical considerations, what you wear on your head is totally up to you, of course. I was most comfortable with wigs. Well, wigs, or nothing at all. I did try various options. I had scarves, but for the life of me, couldn't get them to stay very well on my head. I had a few hats, knitted for someone going through cancer without hair, but they felt itchy, so I didn't wear them all that often.

There are a variety of styles of hats available for women going through cancer. An important consideration is the material: not only is it comfortable, but will the material truly keep the sun off your head? I

> **Donna**
>
> *I am thrilled to discover a wonderful benefit to wigs! My big issue with rain has always been my hair. Everyday I would curl my hair and use an entire bottle of hair spray so it wouldn't go anywhere, only to walk out in rainy weather and have it become a complete sticky mess.*
>
> *But, get this idea....I don't have to put the wig on until I am in the car or at my destination! Wonderful hair even in bad weather. Is this a benefit or what?*

bought one, thinking a hot pink hat with sparkles would be fun, and tried it with a halo, little strips of hair that you put on underneath your cap to give the appearance of having a full head of hair.

Still, I never wore my pink sparkly baseball cap. It just wasn't me.

My preference was wigs, due in large part to the fact that I felt "normal," whatever that might be, when I had hair on my head. I became very comfortable over time, wearing wigs outside and to events. I would go bald-headed in the house, though, I often had a wig nearby in case someone stopped by!

Why Do You Cover Your Head?

Whether you wear a hat, a scarf, or a wig, why do you cover your head? To a large extent, you cover it for those around you. Hair is very important to a woman, as it is a unique expression of herself as a lady. So, when someone doesn't have hair, something seems wrong. Friends and family know you are sick, but seeing you without something on your head makes it so profound for them.

It took me a while to understand that wearing a wig when I was with other people, for me, was important to feeling like a lady. But, importantly, I was also "protecting" others from the ravages of this disease by keeping a wig on my head.

Nowhere was this more evident than when I saw a child. On one occasion, a friend stopped by with her two-year-old. I didn't have my wig on, and the child became petrified; she burst into tears, backed away, and reached for her mother. A child will cry, but will your friend? Probably not, to protect you. So, even at home I wore wigs, to protect them.

I kept one near the front door, so that if someone arrived unexpectedly, I could throw it on as I opened the door. Even this system eventually broke down, though. Some friends thought I was making great headway when halfway through chemo I started answering doors without a wig. Actually, I was so sick at that point that I just didn't have the energy to put it on correctly. And then, I got to a point where I unlocked the door in the morning so people could come and go at will, but more on this later.

Being a lady through cancer is very much about attitude. Although we all know that our hair plays a critical role in how we feel about ourselves, though you will lose it, you can still feel like a lady. You have options. Try a wig, a scarf, a hat, or nothing at all. And see what works for you.

THE REST OF YOUR HAIR

When you think of losing your hair, you think of losing the hair on the top of your head. What you may not expect is that you will lose ALL of your hair, and I do mean ALL.

The hair on your legs. Gone. Under your arms. Gone. Losing this hair, though, is good news, as you don't have to shave for a while and, truly, how awesome is that?

You also lose your nose hair, and while not a very ladylike topic, this loss can actually be a bit of a challenge. The hair in your nose keeps mucous in and other stuff out. Without this hair, you can inhale all sorts of little germs and other irritants. Expect to have a constantly runny nose, keeping those Puffs close at hand, and for your sense of smell to change without those little nose hair filters.

I just have to be honest with you. This is not the only hair you lose. You may very well lose the hair "down there." Yes, you know what we are referring to here. I know, really, who would ever tell you this? It comes out like the rest of your hair a little at a time. You realize one day that your hair is not nearly as dense. Then you wake up to a Brazilian, and just think, no waxing was involved. You are now as clean as a baby.

When we think of hair, we typically think of the hair on our head. But, your treatments are acting on all of your hair, and it is helpful to understand that everything may be impacted.

In a final note, lest you be concerned, losing your hair is not physically painful. It is not as if it is being pulled out. It just falls out. You will not feel it. I share this, because some of this hair loss may come as a surprise. Knowing what might happen so that you are prepared can help you live like a lady.

WHERE TO GO FOR SUPPORT

There are many resources available to you as you go through hair loss. A great place to start is your cancer treatment center. While they may not have wigs, hats, and scarves, themselves, they frequently have lists of places in the area do. Treatment center social workers can also provide this type of information and support as well.

Wig shops, like mine, often have a little salon where they can cut or shave your hair. They typically have great experience with cancer patients and can advise you well on the type of wigs and other items to consider. They are also typically very safe and understanding environments as you go through the journey of losing your hair. If you are going to try the wig path, do not shop online for your first wig. Go to a shop live and try some on to see what is comfortable and right for you. The specialists will show you how to get the wig on correctly and help determine what type of wig will work best for your needs. There are so many choices, not just color and style, but type of hair, etc. Often these wig shops also have some hats and the halos mentioned earlier.

Depending on the type of wig you purchase, they can get rather expensive. However, talk with your wig provider as many times insurance will cover a wig for cancer patients. There are many resources that will provide a wig free of charge to cancer patients, including the Cancer Support Community and Gilda's Club. You can find these and many other resources listed on the Living Like A Lady website at LivingLikeALady.com.

DRY, DRY, DRY

The cancer and chemo do take an enormous toll on our bodies. And true, I had to work everyday to feel like a lady. No denying, it can be a little difficult to feel beautiful and ladylike when you wake up to no hair, puffiness, and brown spots. Yet, I wouldn't let the reflection in the mirror define me. I had to define me. So, what does that look like?

The first thing I noticed, within a week or so of starting chemo, was how dry my skin, and really everything, became. If I hadn't always been good about moisturizing my face and lips at night, I became vigilant about it during chemo, if anything because they began to crack and they hurt. I did learn that you can find that external beauty again; it just takes a little know-how.

To begin with, your skin is your largest organ, and this organ will really take a beating through some of your treatments. So, let's discuss the beating it will take and what you can do about it, starting with your face.

When you wake up and see your bloated face, or puffy eyes, or brown spots, your natural inclination is to pull out the make-up and cover everything up. But, your skin is the foundation for everything, so start there!

You have heard it before, but it can't be said too often: drink lots and lots of water! You need to rehydrate your body, your cells, and water is the simplest, easiest way to do that.

When it comes to your skin, whatever you do, be gentle! Your skin is dry from chemo, medication, radiation, or a combination of these.

Let's start with your chemo. It is killing fast growing cells, and, unfortunately, your skin cells are fast growing. So, while the chemo is doing a number on your tumor, it is also slowing down your ability to produce new skin cells, causing the dryness.

The radiation you might receive, even though it is targeted to something within your body, will still burn your skin in the process. You won't see a burn the first few days or even weeks, but once it hits, ouch! And we know that burnt skin is dry skin. Now, on top of that, depending upon when your chemo treatment is, realize that you may have burnt skin from radiation that is not healing quickly because of the chemo.

You are also likely to be on quite a few medications through your cancer treatments. Some of the meds may be to combat the side effects of the chemo or radiation. Regardless of what you are on, be very careful. Many medications will make your skin much more susceptible to sunburn. Some medications dry out the skin in and of themselves. So, your skin might be dealing with the triple whammy of chemo, radiation, and medication. Thus our mantra: Be gentle!

> **Donna**
>
> *I thought I would "philosophize" a bit on cancer vs. chemo. My Aunt Barb and Uncle Larry sent me a fun card on this topic (thank you!), and here is what I am learning.*
>
> *First of all, cancer doesn't hurt. I never felt it, until I felt the lump, of course. I didn't know I had it, nothing had changed, I felt fine! Well – I was tired, but heck that could be from a bunch of different things. I now know it probably was due to cancer, but it wasn't like I was especially more tired than usual.*
>
> *Chemo, however, is another story. Chemo makes you feel just bad. There are enough medicines to keep you (well, me) from feeling nauseated. But, there are so many side effects from total exhaustion to lack of taste, lack of appetite, acid (even with just water), and others I have already mentioned. (Did I mention I lost my hair? Just checking.)*
>
> *I say this because my natural inclination is to hate chemo, when, really, it is the cancer I should hate. So, I have been telling myself that chemo is my "friend". I can't hate it; I have to love it. In fact, I think I have to give in to it – go ahead and be sick, be tired, and know that by my giving in, it can do its job and kick the cancer.*

Now, no thinking that all is lost! We ladies can wear horribly high heels and dance all night, so we can handle this painful skin. And yes, it is painful. But with a few simple tips and tricks, you can get through this, living like a lady as you do. Of course, drink your water, water, water, no matter what else you do. It is essential!

Cleansing Your Face

Cleansing your face the right way is important, and it probably means changing some things you have always done. Many of us scrub our face, trying to get rid of make-up and prevent break-outs, but, now is the time to be gentle! So put away that Clarisonic, no more apricot scrubs, and no more brushes. Use a really simple, fragrance-free cleanser to remove your make-up. Remember to pat your face gently with a soft washcloth or cotton pad as you do so.

You may have a cleanser that you "swear" by. But, be careful with those. Some have acne control medications in them that will dry out your skin. Avoid cleansers made for oily skin for the same reason because, to combat oiliness, the cleansers are designed to dry out your skin. When you are healthy, that is what you need them to do. But, now, that extra drying factor may not be helpful to you.

Did I say be gentle as you clean your face? Just checking.

Lotions And Potions

After you have gently washed your face, you will want to apply a cream. Again, keep it fragrance free and chemical free. Put it on while your skin is still a little damp so you can seal in the moisture.

Choose a cream over a lotion. Creams tend to have been whipped and are a bit more solid than lotions, so they retain the moisture in the skin better. If you have struggled with oily skin in the past, consider a lighter or whipped cream. However, if you already had dry skin when you were healthy, consider a more solid cream as that will be more hydrating for your skin. Regardless of which direction you go with face cream, do not forget your sunblock! A 50-70 sunblock is recommended, and always put it on last, after any other face cream.

It is always advisable to purchase new face cream, simply to minimize the risk of infection from those previously contaminated products. Most women use their fingers to apply cream. Now, the slightest little contaminant could give you an infection. So, to be better safe than sorry, purchase new and try to keep it germ free by getting it out of the container using Q-tips that you can then just throw away.

While we are on the subject of your face, let's talk lips. For me and many others I talked to, dry lips during treatments were a common problem. Of course, lips get dry anyway, so it stands to reason that as your body gets dry, your lips take a beating. I ended up with a lip balm in every room. The days I felt the worst through treatments were the days my lips bothered me the most, so having a lip balm nearby was helpful. Again, look for fragrance-free, simple pure products that contain more lubricants than parabens. Why you ask? Think of parabens as a seal, keeping moisture in your lips. If there is no moisture in your lips, and they are already dry, the seal will not allow additional moisture to penetrate and help your lips. It, in fact, will make them dryer. You don't need that.

I Am So Tired

Leaving make-up on one or two nights was the extent of my "rebelliousness". Truth be told, I would be quite tired at night. Yet, taking off make-up and putting on cream not only helped the skin, but also made me feel better as well. I was still a lady, despite what I saw on the outside.

That being said, exhaustion will get the best of you once in a while. If you can hardly lift your head, try to find the energy to clean your face and put on night cream. In the morning, when you are still exhausted, simply pat your face with water and apply your moisturizing cream.

The Rest Of Your Skin

Of course you want to keep all of your skin clean, but be careful in your choice of product and process as your skin will be dry all over.

Donna

Ok...so I had to share that I can be a real rebel when the world calls for it.

From my perspective, the news yesterday of yet another surgery justified a little "rebel" attitude.

What did I do? I went to bed without taking my make-up off! I kid you not. And I felt so much better - seriously!

Now you know I stick to the rules in a major way. The rules say you take your make-up off every night before bed. So, did I live large or what last night?

Today I am back in the saddle - ready to tackle the next surgery on Tuesday!

Love to all...

Find fragrance free, non-deodorized, gentle soaps or gels. (Gels may be easier to use, and they don't leave a residue on your skin.) Your body is being challenged by so many different chemicals and changes, so try to keep everything else as simple, pure and gentle as you can. In fact, you may want to purchase several soft and inexpensive white washcloths. Why white? Because white cloths won't have dyes and colors that could irritate your sensitive skin. In addition, if you do get nauseous, white cloths are easily disinfected.

You've heard this before, but this time, really and truly pat yourself dry, don't rub. Rubbing your skin dry may irritate and even scratch it. When you bathe, avoid long, hot showers and baths. Truth be told, I so love a long hot shower, but as I went through treatment, even the heat of a shower could exhaust me, so I found myself naturally turning down the water temperature. And, of course, I had no hair to wash, so I was out in a jiffy.

After you bathe, apply a gentle, fragrance-free non-paraffin lotion to the body. You are looking for deeply hydrating and lubricating lotions that can help with the dryness. Why non-paraffin? Many lotions have paraffin – or wax - which is designed to hold moisture in your skin. However, if your skin is dry and lacking moisture, that paraffin will now prevent moisture from hydrating your skin. One brand that my doctors recommended to me is Eucerin. Readily available and very gentle, it was easy and comfortable to use.

I say "try" to apply lotion right out of the bath because sometimes a shower so wore me out that I would have to rest before I put on lotion. But, so be it. Rest a few minutes, put on lotion, get dressed, and rest a little bit more. Lastly, before you are completely ready for the day, apply your sunblock. Again, look for 50 to 70 sunblock and consider purchasing a spray that is designed for babies. It is easy to apply and usually as gentle and pure as possible for tender skin.

A word about shaving. An advantage of losing your hair is that you won't have to shave, and that is a plus because your skin is

already so irritated. If
you do still have to shave,
invest in an electric razor
as you are less likely to
nick yourself. The slightest
little nick puts you at risk
of infection, that dreaded
word. Follow any shave

> **Donna**
> *Now, another un-ladylike side effect is
> bloody noses. I haven't had those since I was
> what, 5 years old. I am not going to spell
> it out, but think head cold, stuffy nose and
> sniffling while you are wrestling with a bloody
> nose. Nuff said right - cause it is just NOT
> ladylike!! And for the curious, yes, another call
> to the doctor as I am still struggling with this
> very unladylike cold! :-)*

with a gentle, fragrance-free lotion that contains aloe.

Really, That Gets Dry?

Some of the drying aspects are just darn annoying. For instance, if
your body gets dried out, that means your nose is dried out as well.
So, nosebleeds were common occurrences for me. A nose spray mist,
Ocean Nasal Spray, was recommended and helped me. Now, there
are many nose sprays out there, but make sure you confer with your
doctor. Some contain active ingredients, which may not help your
situation. The nose spray is primarily to add moisture back into
your nose, so a simple saline may work best. The nose spray helped,
but I still always had tissue with me, just in case.

Much like you keep lip
balm throughout the
house, keep hand cream
around as well, a gentle,
fragrance-free cream with
no active ingredients.
Active ingredients
stimulate the skin to shed

> **Judy**
> *My team of doctors all worked together and
> answered any and all questions I had for them.
> So I didn't hesitate to ask why everyone failed to
> mention to me that with my fabulous Brazilian
> I received thanks to my chemo cocktail, it would
> also dry me out down there. Past the point of being
> uncomfortable. It was painful! And it stole my
> sex drive! Luckily my husband is very supportive,
> and we try different things to keep the spice in our
> marriage when I can't bring myself to have sex.*

its outer layer more quickly. Because of your treatment, though, your skin is slow to regenerate itself. So, such a cream could actually make your skin dryer.

You also are likely to wash your hands more often as you go through treatment, trying to make sure you are fighting those pesky germs. That is the right thing to do! But, your hands will get even drier, so prepare for that with multiple hand creams around the house.

Now, at the risk of getting a bit personal, when I say everything gets dry, I do mean everything! A friend going through chemo told me that on a day or two when she was feeling great, she and her husband wanted to have a little fun between the sheets. It was just too painful. The reason, she was way too dry "down there." So, if you are considering an intimate evening with your partner, remember to make sure you have a lubricant on hand. Astroglide is a commonly recommended brand. You want it to be an enjoyable evening, not a painful one.

> **Judy**
> I had absolutely no sex drive during treatment, and my vagina became drier moreso after treatment had ended. I am estrogen positive and cannot take a replacement to help balance things out down there, so I am forced to use over the counter lubricants that do not work very well. I use Recleanse. It is estrogen free and has worked the best for me. Treatment also threw my 40 year old body into menopause, and my lining started to thin, which makes it very painful down there. (All of the time, not just during sex.) I was prescribed Estrace, a local cream that is inserted to ease the pain and help keep elasticity in the lining. I could use this because it is a local and not a pill that goes into your blood stream. The Recleanse and Estrace combo helps.

As you can see, when we say everything gets dry, we really mean it. The dryness is not limited to your skin. My eyes were so dry that I couldn't wear my contacts during most of my treatment. I would put them in if I was going out and could last perhaps an hour at most and I had to remove them. Of course, putting contacts in and taking them out puts you at risk of infection. So, I had to ask myself, was it really worth it to put them in for an hour?

If you are comfortable with your glasses, just wear those. If not, talk with your eye doctor to see what drops he or she might recommend. For me, drops just didn't seem to help enough, so I mostly went without my contacts.

A lot more on fingernails later, but in terms of dryness, they will suffer as well. Keep Solar Oil nearby to rub into your cuticles.

DRY MOUTH

Another potentially serious issue as you go through chemo is dry mouth. The chemo can damage your salivary glands while it kills those cancer cells. If this happens, you may not produce as much, if any, saliva. Without saliva, your mouth gets dried out, potentially causing sores to develop and something as simple as eating and drinking to really hurt. Because you are already at risk for not eating and drinking as much when you go through chemo, you don't want mouth sores to escalate the problem for you.

Your doctors may be very concerned with dry mouth, so, of course listen to their recommendations on this critical issue and follow their advice. I was advised to gargle with a solution I made at home for a few days after chemo treatments. Another product often recommended for gargling is Biotin.

Of course, I didn't really see gargling as a very ladylike thing to do. However, gargling as recommended kept my mouth clean and somewhat moist, and I never did develop any mouth sores.

Don't Forget

So now you know, when I say dry, dry, dry, I do mean all over. From your skin to your nose to your mouth to your eyes, treatment may really dry you out. How much you get dried out depends on you: your body, your treatment, and how pro-active you are.

I will say it again: Drink your water! That is so critical. But, don't forget to treat your skin with gentle, loving care. Dry skin easily cracks, gets injured and potentially infected, and that can lead to an entirely new set of challenges. Keep moisturizers, lip balms, and hand creams easily accessible, and you may be able to limit the discomfort of dryness from your treatments.

BURN, BURN, BURN

Gosh did I struggle with how to handle this chapter on radiation. So much of radiation impacts your skin, so shouldn't it be in the Dry, Dry, Dry chapter on skin? Yet, radiation is its own special treatment, with particular side effects. So, perhaps it needed to stand on its own. In the end, I decided the sequel to Dry, Dry, Dry would be Burn, Burn, Burn, as the two are so related.

Radiation is a critical treatment for many cancers. Often it is done in coordination with other treatments, such as surgery or chemo. The role of radiation is rather specific. It is designed to kill the cancer cells in a very targeted

---

Donna

What a crazy day today was. Let me explain. I met with the radiology oncologist, and after providing some basic information, she says, "Look, your cancer is completely curable - but it is really bad. You had a large tumor - 10 total cm - and you are Her positive, which is the most aggressive type of breast cancer." (So, in fairness, I knew all of this - I just didn't share it with everyone.) As a result, she wants to start radiation immediately, and by the way, there is no choice on the whole radiation thing. I am getting it!

Well, then she takes a look at the whole surgery site. My heavens she had NEVER seen anything like that before. (Because of the way it was healing, it looked like I had four perky girls, not just two.) But, my plastic surgeon is the best, as the oncologist confirmed, and she will get it figured out for me. I explain that surgery was just moved again to Thursday to get everything corrected. Well, the radiation oncologist didn't like that, because that is going to delay when my radiation can start.

Now, on a side note: Why radiation, when we have so much good news about the tumor shrinking and then being totally removed by the mastectomy? Well, radiation will be directed at the breast, lymph nodes, and throat – any place the cells could have migrated. Because of the size and the fast growing type of cancer, I have to do radiation to ensure no cancer cells have tried to start growing again. At least, that is my understanding of it!

So, what to do, what to do, what to do - continue with surgery and make me not so disfigured? Or, postpone surgery and start radiation? I don't know the correct answer. The doctors had to put their heads together to determine the best course of action.

Later that afternoon I receive the call. We are proceeding with the understanding that I will have more surgery. We will begin radiation most likely several weeks after that. Radiation will continue for 28 straight days (excluding weekends). I will start OT and PT again on my arms about a week after surgery.

21

and specific manner. Of course, in the killing of cancer cells, it also has the ability to damage you, causing everything from burns to fatigue.

Treatment Course

A course of radiation treatment is handled very differently from a course of chemo treatment. Typically, radiation occurs every day and may last from as little as a week for Mammosite to as long as six or eight weeks. As we so often see, it depends: Breast brachytherapy may occur two times a day for five days while more traditional radiation protocols may be once a day for several weeks.

You will find that radiation treatments most often run like clockwork. You get there, get changed, get called back, the treatment may last 10 to 15 minutes, and then you are finished. During your course of treatment, you will likely meet with your radiation oncologist once a week to monitor how you are tolerating your treatment, including side effects, and determine how effectively the treatment is working.

Many people schedule their treatment for the same time everyday, although that doesn't have to be the case. One advantage I found to having the regular schedule is that I got to know others going through radiation. There is something reassuring about being with the same group of people everyday, and then celebrating when someone has finished her course of treatment.

In order to prepare you for treatment, your radiation oncology team may have you come in ahead of time so that you can be "set up." I had an impression of my head, neck, and shoulder taken while lying down. A form was created from that, and for each treatment, my head, neck, and shoulder had to be perfectly positioned in the form to ensure that the treatment was in the exact same location each time.

After the form was created, another "dry run" session was done to "mark" me. Some markings are done with a black marker. Mine were actually pinpoint tattoos that were applied. The form keeps the body part from moving while the radiologist uses the markings to guide the radiation to the exact right spot each time.

Getting you situated in the right position for each radiation treatment often takes longer than the actual treatment, which can go rather quickly. Be forewarned that the machine makes a noisy, pulsing sound that is unsettling for some people; however, on the plus side, you typically will not feel any pain or discomfort.

I did experience a complication that, while not common, was not insurmountable. As the physicists (PhDs in nuclear physics are important people in your treatment) set me up, they realized that, based on where they needed to radiate for the tumor, the radiation would hit my heart on the way, which, of course, they did not want to do. I did find out that this occurs with left breast cancer patients about 20 percent of the time. To avoid the heart, they inflate the lungs, which moves the heart out of the way as radiation takes place, a clever solution.

> **Donna**
>
> *Hmmmm....what to call this post! The Road Less Travelled...Again! That is an option. What about... It's Always Something! Oh, how about...I Can't Really Make This Up.... Or, maybe we should call it...**An Affair of the Heart**...*
>
> *Oh, wait, you want to know what happened, don't you! Well, today I was supposed to get prepared and ready for radiation. So, I headed to the radiation oncologist to get this thing rolling. She explained everything and I headed to get prepped. They lay you in the machine and make a form of your shoulders. I will lie in that each time, so that I am precisely in the same position.*
>
> *They had my left arm (cancer side) above my head and my right arm (sore side) by my side. They struggled and struggled to get the measurements right. (Usually both arms are above your head, but with my shoulder problem, they can't do that.) They measured, taped, marked. They called in, ultimately, three nuclear physicists to make sure everything was positioned correctly. They thought they had it sorted out, and they took the CAT scan. They do that to make sure everything is precisely where it needs to be before they use the laser beams. (I wasn't going to get the real beam today - we were just setting up.)*
>
> *So, after 45 minutes of keeping my arms in very awkward positions, the doctor came back in. You know something is up when she sits on the radiation table right next to you. Well, she said, I knew from the moment I met you that you had a large heart, a special heart. But, I didn't expect that it would be in a different place. No, it's not in my big toe! But, apparently, it is a little bit more to the center of my chest - not on the left side. Well, that is a problem, because they really don't want to radiate my heart! That would be a bad thing. And, based on the location of my heart they can't radiate me with this equipment. So, what to do? I will head to the David Pratt Cancer Center at Mercy Hospital tomorrow, and we will see if I can do it there. They have equipment that can get around the heart when this occurs.*

To inflate my lungs, I had to take a deep breath and hold it for a few seconds, so that they could give me the radiation with my heart out of the way. Typically radiation is done continuously for a few minutes and then you are done. In my case, it could only be done in little increments, allowing me to breathe in between and then continue. Because one of my significant side effects from chemo and the Herceptin I was on was shortness of breath, I couldn't hold my breath very long. As a result, my treatment sessions took longer than most people experience.

For the 20 percent of you who may have to experience a machine helping you to hold your breath, as I did, let me say it is very disconcerting, especially in the beginning. However, as treatment progressed, I became very accustomed to it and it became tolerable.

Donna

So, I can see a group of engineers sitting around a table. "Houston, we have a problem....how do we radiate cancerous tissue without getting the heart? Especially when the heart is misplaced....?"

Follow me through this imagined engineering conversation....to find out how my day went!

"Well, the last thing we want to do is radiate the heart."

"Yes, we are seeing side effects show in 10 to 20 years as heart problems - and this troublemaker is young. She'll be with us a while, so I guess we should avoid potential heart side effects with her."

"So, we have to figure out how to move the heart out of the way."

"I've got it...let's NOT move the heart, let's move everything else!"

"What do you mean?"

"Well, if you inflate the lungs, that pushes the old breast tissue up and out of the way. Then we treat that tissue, and it is far enough from the heart that we do no damage."

"Awesome idea! The lung will act like a balloon and keep everything expanded. So, how do we do that to a patient and keep the lung expanded for 15 minutes or so for the radiation?"

"Uh, people," says the Indiana University MD, "the patient needs to breath! Try 15 seconds instead!"

"Oh, yeah, oh yeah," comes the chorus from the engineers.

"Well, let's have her take a really deep breath and hold it."

"How can we be sure she holds it?"

"Let's put a snorkle type device on her. Once she blows up her lungs, we will turn a valve so that the lungs stay inflated, and she can't breath out."

"Perfect...now we are getting somewhere!"

"Uh, guys, what about her nose? Won't air come out her nose??"

"I know, I know," says the Purdue Engineer named Al. "Why don't we put a clamp on her nose; then she can't breath at all! "

"Woo Hoo....I think we've got it!"

And yep...that is how it works! Clamp on my nose, snorkle in my mouth - everything hooked up to computers. I take a deep breath, and the computer takes over...a VERY WEIRD experience, may I say. But it is going to work....

They will have me do this about five times for 8 to 10 seconds every time I have radiation. They will radiate only when my lungs are inflated. What if I get a cold or the flu? We'll cross that bridge when we get to it they said. I can always hope that my nose gets stuffed up, so I don't need that clamp!

They will take pictures on Friday to make sure everything is lined up and working well. Monday we will start the radiation!

Here's to the engineers who you just know were involved in solving this little challenge, the first time this approach was used!

Love to all...

SIDE EFFECTS

Radiation is known for its side effects, especially the burn. Others include significant fatigue, hair loss, infections, and lymphedema. For each, you can take measures that still allow you to live radiantly, while you go through radiation treatment.

Burn

Radiation burn is common; nonetheless, it needs to be handled very carefully. As the radiation kills tumor cells, it also burns the skin cells. Unfortunately, your skin, while fast growing, cannot keep up with the pace that the radiation damages it. You may begin to see some slight changes to your skin, such as redness or little spots or bubbles, after the first week of treatment or so. Often, the worse parts of the burn are towards the end of treatment and even a few weeks post treatment. As is so often the case, when you see and how much of an impact you see depends. It depends on where your

> **Donna**
>
> *Now, what to expect with radiation...this time people are telling me! I think the doctors are concerned that I could have a hard time, primarily because I have had every reaction possible to everything else done.*
>
> *My hope is that now that they are telling me what might happen, none of it will!*
>
> *So, the one fear is fatigue. Also, a sunburn-like redness, although I have been warned about blisters, sores, infections, and even charred or black skin! But please, I can handle anything for 28 days - right? That is the length of my treatment.*
>
> *Speaking of handling anything - I plan to work through this. Unless I am exhausted, why not work! Also, I am still taking the Herceptin, and I get that Thursday. So, I could be facing a bit of an exhausting weekend.*
>
> *Lots of love to everyone...and more updates to come as we enter phase three....*

cancer is, how your radiation oncologist is treating it, and what other treatments you may already have had or will have.

Radiation oncology teams often recommend Aquaphor to treat your burn. In the beginning, when my skin first turned red, that was the product to use. I soon learned to buy it by the tub and use it liberally as it did really help to calm the skin, relieve the burn, and speed the healing. Be exceptionally careful when applying Aquaphor or any other product that your doctor recommends. The skin is so highly sensitive and damaged at this point that it does not take much to really hurt it or scratch it. Scratches, in particular, can lead to infection.

I was advised to use plastic gloves when applying the Aquaphor as it is greasy and difficult to wash

> **Donna**
>
> *Went to my radiation session (aka sunburn session) well prepared! I brought along my Banana Boat SPF 30 sunscreen. Darn, they wouldn't let me use it, but, they did all laugh! :-)*
>
> *The doctor can't believe I have an effect already! She is guessing I might be allergic to the detergent they use on hospital gowns. We'll watch it and see. I say I'll do anything to get out of those ugly things! :-)*
>
> *Love,*

off. Use of gloves also limits contamination. Consider using a long tongue depressor (popsicle stick) to apply the product. The burned areas may be difficult to reach, and this gives you a better chance of applying it well, but be exceptionally careful. After you have applied the product, wrap the area with gauze. I found myself applying Aquaphor multiple times a day; as I woke up, before bed, and several times in between. Steer clear of using adhesive, band aids, even paper tape, etc., to hold the gauze and Aquaphor in place. Wearing a soft but fitted shirt can do the job. Large, soft, compression sleeves can also hold the gauze. Check with your doctor and radiation nurses on this. They often have ideas on what has worked for others.

I was advised not to wear a bra at this time. Fortunately, with expanders in, I did not have to wear one anyway. Expanders are temporary devices that stretch your skin slowly in preparation for implants. If you do need to wear a bra, you may want to consider more of a sports type style with no wire as that can be rather irritating.

Wherever the radiation is being targeted is subject to being burned, which usually starts off looking red, much like a sunburn. Your burnt area may change colors and appearance as your treatments progress. Mine went from red to a deep red to almost purple, and I was told that skin can even turn black, although mine did not. I share not to scare you, but so that you are aware that it is possible. It probably goes without saying that as the skin changes color, it becomes more and more painful. When my skin was deep red and purple, I learned of the technique with the tongue depressor to apply Aquaphor as it was very uncomfortable to move and reach all of the burned areas.

Along with the burn comes dryness, even to the point of skin flaking off (much like

> **Donna**
>
> *Radiation went fine, the only issue being my breathing.*
>
> *You see, this whole Herceptin thing I got on Thursday - one of the side effects is shortness of breath. That doesn't work so well when you are supposed to hold your breath.*
>
> *Another question to ponder - how many muscles does it take to hold your breath? Well, if you are me, apparently all of them! Like, why do my feet rise off the table when I am holding my breath? Because, dog-gone it, I will not, I repeat, NOT let the breath out too soon. And, every ounce of my body will be involved to make sure that doesn't happen!*
>
> *One of the best things I did today was to ask the radiation nurses if I could have wine! Thank heavens they said that they encourage it!!!*

> **Donna**
>
> *One interesting aspect of radiation is that they put a wet towel over the left side of my chest halfway through the radiation. Apparently, there is such a thin layer of muscle between the expander and the skin that the radiation beam actually ends up focusing on the expander instead of the muscle and skin tissue. But, by putting a wet towel on me, they "fake" the machine into delivering the radiation at the right location.*

a traditional sunburn). You skin can become exceptionally itchy. Try to avoid scratching at all costs as not only will it hurt, but it will also introduce the chance for bacteria and infection. Do speak with your doctor if you are having issues with your treatment area being itchy as he or she may have other topical medications that can alleviate that sensitivity. Aquaphor will not really address this issue.

Another important skin issue to look out for is wet or moist skin, especially in areas where there are skin folds, such as underneath your breast, your neck, or behind your ears. Ulcers or sores can form in these areas due to the friction, and this can lead to significant infections.

Taking care of your skin during treatment follows many of the same guidelines we discussed in the chapter Dry, Dry, Dry. To begin with, keep your radiated area out of the sun; you want no direct sun exposure on your skin during radiation. In fact, once an area has had radiation, it will always be extra sensitive to sun and will be at greater risk of skin cancer, so you will always want to be extra protective there. During your treatment keep it covered, but also consider always applying a good SPF of 50 just in case. I quickly learned that while my breast was being radiated, the radiation may also have been hitting parts of my neck, making it more susceptible to burns as well. Be cognizant that any type of SPF lotion can be irritating to radiated skin. Sunscreen designed for babies is your best bet. Importantly, wearing clothes that cover and protect that delicate skin from the sun will be most crucial.

Also as I discuss in Dry, Dry, Dry, remember to take lukewarm showers or baths, not hot or cold, which can be very irritating to this damaged skin. Also, remember to pat your skin, not rub or scrub it.

Use mild or fragrance free soaps as they will be less irritating. Do be very careful NOT to wash off any of the markings that the radiation team has put on you for your treatment. In my case, the tattoos, of course, would not wash off, but for others, the permanent ink can wash off if you are not careful.

A note for those being treated around the throat with radiation. Think of the inside of your throat as similar to your skin: That delicate tissue may take a beating. The complications discussed here, from being burnt to being dry, can occur in your mouth and throat as well. Unfortunately, that can become so painful that you don't want to eat or drink, which, of course, leads to other complications. A friend I met at radiation, who was always there at the same time as I, was struggling with throat cancer. While she tried valiantly to get milkshakes and other nutritional products down, she ended up requiring a feeding tube. Unfortunately, this is more common than we like to hear for those with mouths and throats impacted by radiation. Refer to the chapter Being Beautiful On The Outside to learn about dry mouth and the damage that can do to your teeth should your throat and mouth get dry.

While most of the skin side effects are short term, in that they happen right away and eventually clear up, there are some potential long-term skin side effects to consider. Of primary concern is the creation of scar tissue, which can be painful at times but can also limit your movement. Working with an occupational therapist post radiation can help ensure your range of motion is not lost as result of the treatment. Another important skin consideration is that you may lose elasticity. The radiated site will not stretch and move the way it might have in the past. It is this side effect that becomes of significant concern for the breast cancer patient if she is considering reconstruction as it must be done in a coordinated fashion for the best possible result.

Hair Loss

While an entire chapter is dedicated to losing your hair and another dedicated to your hair growing back, it is important to note that you can lose your hair with radiation treatment as with chemotherapy. Typically it falls out in the location of the radiation and

> **Donna**
>
> *Meanwhile, my radiation burns seemed to be getting worse. I know this now marked one week post radiation, but it was getting redder, almost purple in places. Mom's role as nurse was to put dressings on it, which was so helpful as it hurt just to move my arms!*
>
> *Come Thursday night I emailed the plastic surgeon's office. They suggested that I keep following up with them on skin issues, and, I don't know, I just didn't like what was happening here with the burns. FRIDAY - I got a call from the plastic surgeon's office to please come by that afternoon. They didn't like what they were hearing. Sure enough - they thought I had an infection at the radiation site. So, I was put on antibiotics right away.*

not all over, as chemo is apt to do to you. Depending on the type and location of the radiation, it is possible that the hair will not regrow. Talk to your doctor about the type of radiation you will receive and what it means for your hair. For example, I have never regrown hair under the arm that was radiated. Of course, I see that as a plus!

Infection

Infection is a significant complication from radiation and one that you want to

> **Donna**
>
> *One bit of news to report - while I am feeling great, the infection does not seem to be going away quite yet. So, the other day, the doctor put me on a second antibiotic - so two a day. It is hard to tell if it is improving, as I am still so red in general. The really red, almost purply parts, are starting to peel. But, I am finding with a radiation burn, it is not like a typical burn in that it doesn't really peel; it is crispy.*

watch for closely. It can be a little tricky to detect as your skin turns red from the treatment, itself. So, look for additional changes in color, for sores, for anything that looks different. I learned to take photos on my phone of changes in the skin and tissue and email the picture to the nurses or doctors if I was concerned. They were very willing to look at all the pictures I sent and tell me whether what they saw was concerning or normal.

I did end up with a significant infection post radiation, and it took quite a few courses of antibiotics to eliminate it. Why are infections so difficult? If you have had chemo and/ or surgery before radiation, your body is already fatigued and your blood counts may be low, meaning your immune system is compromised. A serious infection can require additional surgery. In the case of the breast cancer patient, such as myself, if we had not addressed the infection quickly, I would have had to have the expanders removed, and the options for reconstruction would have been considerably limited. At this point, you are also probably fatigued from the radiation, and you really don't need one more thing draining your energy, like an infection. To that end, take it seriously, and make sure you keep a watchful eye on your treated area

Donna

Hi Everyone,

The good news is, I am home. The bad news is, I spent most of the day at the hospital. The Herceptin always makes me short of breath, but couple that with radiation, and I have just been gasping today. So, I went to radiation and saw the doctor today. She was quite concerned and sent me to the ER for fear of a blood clot. After another lung CAT scan and another Doppler ultra sound on my leg, they determined no blood clot.

It is just that for me Herceptin and radiation are a bad mix. I will get this double whammy one more time.

In the meantime, a big thank you to my physical therapist and dear friend Bryan. He didn't like what he saw (I tried to do PT today) and took me to radiation and ultimately the hospital today. Bryan, thank you for everything!!

Once again, I am ever thankful for the wonderful friends and angels in my life. And now, I will go to sleep - thankfully in my own bed!

so that you can let your doctors know if something needs additional attention.

Fatigue

Fatigue is a very common side effect with radiation. I devote an entire chapter to fatigue that provides even more detail; however, I found fatigue with radiation to be different from that with chemo or surgery in that it crept up on me. The feeling is the same, the inability to even raise your head at times, but, unlike with chemo where it would come and then go, radiation fatigue got a little worse with each day for me. All of a sudden I realized that driving was exhausting, and that while I could get myself to radiation, simply driving home might be too much.

One thing to note is that fatigue exacerbates whatever other issues you have. Other issues seem much more pronounced. For me, shortness of breath was a constant issue, so that reared its ugly head when I was very fatigued. For others, joint pain or others issues may feel more prevalent. I learned to recognize that an increase in particular symptoms meant that my body was fatigued and that rest was required.

Lymphedema

A very significant side effect that can impact you for the rest of your life is lymphedema, a critical side effect for both surgery and radiation. It can occur whenever there is a disruption to the lymphatic system, which filters and cleans the tissue fluids. With lymphedema, the fluids just settle somewhere and cause swelling, and while it can occur as a result of all sorts of things, there is a greater risk when a lymph node is removed or damaged, which is common with breast cancer surgeries (mastectomies and lumpectomies) and treatments.

The immediate impact of lymphedema is swelling and a decrease in your range of motion. The impact can be mitigated through therapy as soon as possible post surgery and radiation. A physical therapist or occupational therapist who is Lymphology Association of North America (LANA) certified can use massage to move the fluids. He or she can also work on the fibrosis (thickening of tissue, similar to scar tissue) that often occurs due to radiation. Both the fibrosis and the swelling can lead to range of motion limitations, so getting some active assistance early on is critical.

Lymphedema generally works in stages. Stage one typically includes intermittent swelling which you may notice more at night. Stage two is characterized by swelling that does not subside and which progressively gets worse. Stage three is swelling that is not being managed or controlled, typically resulting in pronounced fibrosis and elephantitis (a condition in which the body part becomes very large due to swelling).

In the early stages, lymphedema is managed by massage and a compression sleeve and gauntlet, or glove. These tight sleeves, fitted by a medical specialty shop, force the fluids to move through the body. Remember to wear the gauntlet or hand piece if you wear a sleeve so that your hand doesn't swell at the expense of your arm. If you move into a more advanced stage, you may very well be treated with tight bandaging with a goal of transitioning you into a garment or compression sleeve as the swelling goes down.

Once you have had lymphedema, you are always at risk for it, requiring lifelong vigilance. If you see your lymphedema acting up, you can take steps to correct and manage it. Look for early signs:

a feeling of heaviness or achiness in your extremities, a pulling or tightness in the area, or clothes or jewelry fitting tightly.

There are steps you can take to limit the risk of lymphedema returning or acting up. Importantly, always wear your sleeve when doing any sort of air travel. Check with your therapist, as he or she may want you to wear it at other times as well, such as car trips through the mountains. Hot tubs and saunas can increase the risk, so avoid them or keep your time to a minimum, such as 10 to 15 minutes. If you are in a hot tub, simply keeping the affected arm out of the tub will be an enormous help. Prevent your affected arm (or leg) from having any tight or constricted items around it. For arms, blood pressure cuffs and tight jewelry, for example, can all trigger a lymphedema flare-up. Also, avoid any trauma to the affected side, such as a needle stick. In other words, have blood drawn from the other side. A particular challenge for me is to avoid carrying heavy bags and purses on my left side, where the cancer was.

My lymphedema did come back in a significant way about three years post treatments. A few weeks of wearing my sleeve and gauntlet and visits with my occupational therapist minimized the swelling. I discovered the recurrence of lymphedema while I was working out. My trainer couldn't understand why one arm was not nearly as toned as the other, and I grew suspicious. Sure enough, the lymphedema caused my arms to look different from each other. Still, I was able to keep working out as I was treated for the lymphedema.

Lymphedema can be managed, but this is most effective if you catch it early. You may deal with it for the rest of your life, so be vigilant, and if you see a little change, address it. This will serve you well in the long run!

BEING BEAUTIFUL ON THE OUTSIDE

You try so hard to be radiant, despite this storm swirling around you. While your spirit is willing, and succeeding may we add, your body, on the other hand, is struggling. So, let's discuss some of the things you can do to be beautiful on the outside, from teeth and manicures to make-up. Let's find that outer beauty that reflects your inner radiance.

To begin with, start with a smile. We know you know that, but there is something so beautiful about a woman ravaged by a disease who can still smile. Your inner glow will start to appear, if not through your eyes, through your smile.

Start With Your Smile

When I started my chemo, I was quickly told by my oncologist not to go to the dentist. The reason was simple. The mouth has a large amount of bacteria, and even a routine thing like a cleaning could result in an infection. It never occurred to me to call the dentist and let him know that I had cancer and was starting chemo treatments. Oh, how I wish I had known to call him.

I received my chemo through a port inserted into my neck so that the drug could be delivered directly into my bloodstream. Regardless of the delivery system, a port or pills, a phone call to your dentist to let him or her know you are receiving chemo may save you great angst later on.

Chemo, being chemo, kills off all sorts of things, including the ability for salivary glands to produce saliva. My mouth was so dry during the chemo. Saliva, as I learned the hard way, is very important in the protection of your teeth. Now, I realize that a discussion on saliva is not necessarily a "lady-like" topic; however, a beautiful smile is. So, let's "grin" and bear it on this issue so that you don't face the challenges I did.

Treatment for cancer, no matter where it is in the body, can affect teeth, gums, salivary glands, and other tissues of the mouth. As a lady going through cancer, being vigilant about side effects in your mouth, such as mouth sores, dry mouth, gum disease, and tooth decay, can help to keep your smile bright. Having your dentist on board, as I only learned later, can be invaluable in keeping your mouth healthy.

Basically, dry mouth (or Xerostomia) is when your salivary glands do not work properly. Saliva is vital to tasting, swallowing, speaking, and digesting and is a natural defense against tooth decay and bacterial, fungal, and viral infections. It is composed primarily of water but also includes electrolytes, mucus, antibacterial compounds, and various enzymes. These components are critical in keeping your mouth healthy as they rinse away food particles, neutralize harmful acids, and actually provide the enzymes that start your overall digestive process.

A call to your dentist can really help you manage dry mouth and its effect. Your dentist may recommend brushing your teeth more frequently and using an ultra-soft toothbrush so as not to damage your gums. Flossing is always important, but if there are areas of soreness or bleeding of your gums, you may be advised to floss very gently or even avoid that area. As I discuss in the chapter on What to Pack for an Emergency Trip to the Hospital, blood issues can be challenging during chemo, so, be gentle to your gums so they don't bleed.

Because your sense of taste will change, in part from the lack of saliva production, you may prefer a very mild tasting toothpaste that also will be less likely to irritate your mouth. You may also want to consider an antibacterial mouth rinse for gum disease, though avoid those containing alcohol as they have a drying effect. From recommendations on prescription toothpastes and mouthwashes to diet changes that may relieve the symptoms, your dentist can provide information that can help. Inform your dentist when you discover your cancer; be your own advocate for your beautiful smile.

For my part, I finished my treatments in about a year and was finally told I could return to the dentist, and oh what a disappointment. It turned out that I needed four crowns, all on the right side, the same as my port. The saliva production, especially on the side of the port, had really been damaged during chemo. The dentist explained that had I called him, he could have prescribed a toothpaste, such as Flouridex, that might have helped protect my teeth during the chemo.

By three years post diagnosis, the dentist was happy with my "saliva production" as it returned to normal. But, I am still vigilant, and still on prescription toothpaste, just to make sure I don't have any other problems with my pearly whites.

MAKE-UP

Ok, you are smiling. You look in the mirror, though, and sigh "oh my." I know. Your hair is gone, your face is bloated from the drugs, and there are brown spots you are not used to seeing. I have talked about it before, but when I say you may lose all your hair, you may lose ALL your hair, including eyebrows and eyelashes, and you may even lose

39

your fingernails. I used to joke that I knew why God took my hair with chemo; it gave me more time to do all the make-up I needed to do.

So, let's tackle these issues. First of all, let's discuss the why of what you are seeing. As you go through your chemo, you most likely will be placed on steroid medications to treat your cancer, limit inflammation, and, often, prevent nausea from chemo. They are common with chemo drugs and are notorious for making you puffy. You may see that puffiness very quickly in your face. Your eyes may look like little slits, though, most likely, it is your face puffing up around your eyes that is causing that look. You may very well be on chemo for a number of weeks or months, which means you may be on steroids for weeks or months at a time. Also, realize that it will take weeks and months for the steroids to move out of your system after you finish them. In other words, it may be weeks and months after you finish all your medications before you will see your face go back to its normal shape and size. In the meantime you can lessen the side effect of puffiness with make-up.

Another effect you are apt to see is lots of brown spots on your face. In general, hormones tend to stimulate the appearance of brown spots. Often hormones have contributed to the development of their cancers (especially breast, ovarian, and cervical). As a result, chemo is used to stimulate or minimize hormones to stop the cancer. Because of that hormonal change, you may see the brown spots appear. Often they are clustered where you have had skin burn or damage in the past from a bit too much sun. The trick again is to cover up the brown spots during your cancer treatments. There are ways to eliminate them more fully, but that is only for after all your cancer treatments.

Since make-up is an important way to camouflage your side effects, let's start with that. To be fair, you may not always feel like putting on your make-up, and that is okay as well.

Donna

Whatever you do Mom and Dad, do NOT read this!! I repeat - do NOT!!! You're still reading it, aren't you? And you wonder where I get my stubbornness from? So, are you stopping now? Ok, good! For the rest of you - please keep this a secret - from you know who — because I will never hear the end of it! You see, I went out to a big party last night and had an absolute blast!

Here is the story. Every year there is a wonderful Arts & Education Council party in January celebrating the best of the arts and those in the art community. I have gone to many of these, and last night was the twentieth anniversary of the gala. Well, my good friend Patty called, and, unfortunately, her friend couldn't make it, and she had an extra ticket. Now, she wasn't asking: I don't want anyone to blame her for this one! I said, gosh I wish I could go, sort of wistfully. Because I do love these types of events and supporting the community.

She agreed that it would be fun. I said, well maybe I can - I mean why not? (Uhhh...the whole cancer and double mastectomy less than two weeks ago thing Donna!) But, let's be real, all we needed was the wig, lots of make-up, and something dressy that would cover the five drainage tubes. (I know you are still reading this Mom and Dad - and shaking your head! But it is ok — really!)

So, I got all gussied up - took me at least two hours to do my make-up. (Had to take some rest breaks, you know.) Found some fun jewelry, put on my long brown tweed cape that I had bought for dressier purposes when I knew surgery and drainage tubes were on the way, and waited for Patty to pick me up.

So, we are halfway there, and Patty begins to panic (I think). OMGosh — what have I done - you are still recuperating. What medicines are you on? Where is your insurance card? What do I need to know?

Okay, Patty, calm down - all will be fine! Here is what you need to know. Do not, I repeat, do NOT let the drains show from under the cape! So, be on drain alert if the cape swings at all. Secondly, try not to let people hug me. The arms and shoulder things still hurt, so "air" kisses will be best for the evening!

For the rest of it, no more than two glasses of wine will be fine, and when I am tired, I will just ever so gracefully (I hope) sit down! Yes, we can do this. We can get dressed, feel good, go to a party and socialize after all this breast cancer stuff. For my part, I felt fantastic! I think I looked pretty good as well, if I may say so! :-)

My favorite comment of the night coming from an old boss, saying wow you look good. How are you? My answer - "you know what, I am absolutely great." And I am....

Love to all!!!

Much like I suggested in the chapter Dry, Dry, Dry with your cleansers and moisturizers, I highly recommend buying new products. Again, you need to minimize the risk of infection, so starting with non-contaminated products is best. Investing in disposable sponges, eye shadow applicators, and Q-tips is another great way of minimizing the risk of infection. Storing your Q-tips, applicators, etc., in a dry, closed container will help to keep them germ free as well. Another little tip: Keep alcohol swabs on hand. If you do get the flu or a cold, you can always wipe off lipsticks, etc., with alcohol swabs to clean them of germs.

The objective of your make-up is to balance out skin tone in order to disguise some of the skin changes. In that spirit, look for high quality products that allow your skin to breath, to get oxygen. Avoid products that are chemically intense, waterproof, or have treatments in them. Again, you want simple, fragrance free products that are both easy to apply and easy to remove. Often, these may be botanical products

An early investment should be a good foundation. Try to match your foundation to your chest skin tone, as that is an easy way to get a most natural looking color for you. The foundation should provide full coverage but should not have any beauty treatments in it with the exception of sun protection factor (SPF). This does not replace your sunblock, however. Make sure you still apply a 50-70 sun block to your face. You don't need a sunburn on top of everything.

Apply your foundation using a disposable sponge. Try to cover your skin with an even amount of foundation. Once the foundation is on and has set, touch up any remaining dark areas or brown spots with a concealer.

On the topic of concealers, be forewarned: You may need two different concealers, one for your brown spots and one for your eyes. For covering the brown spots, typically look for a "rosey" shade, often called "fair" in the make-up lines. Use a spatula to pull out a little of the concealer and apply it to any brown spots you see on your face. Give it a moment to dry a little. Then blot it to blend it in with your skin. Always blot, never wipe. As the saying goes, wiping removes, blotting builds – coverage, that is.

The concealer for your eyes should be two shades lighter than your skin, in a golden tone. The golden color will disguise the purple around your eyes that often comes about because you just simply do not feel well. Again, blot concealer underneath your eye to disguise the dark shadows.

Your goal, as you apply your make-up, should be to enhance your look. You want make-up to appear subtle, but result in a refreshed or luminous quality to your skin. Keep it simple. Avoid the glamorous look for now as the deeper, brighter, and glitzier colors and techniques may emphasize the shadows in your face due to the puffiness from steroids.

As you begin to work on your eyes, it is all the more important to try to avoid amplifying negative shadows. Stay away from grays, cobalt blues, purples, pinks, and greens in eye shadows. Not only can they highlight dark shadows, they may also give a look of bruising. Instead, opt for nudes, apricots, browns, and latte colors. Coupled with a black, dark navy, or dark brown eyeliner, those colors can help your eyes look refreshed and more vibrant.

To make your eyes really pop, add a touch of pearl, non-glittery eye shadow to the inner corners of your eyes and under the natural arch of your brow. This will help them appear open and bright. Of course, a coat or two of non-fibrous mascara, if you still have eyelashes, will complete the look for your eyes. Do not use waterproof mascara as you go through

> **Donna**
>
> *Good Morning All...*
>
> *Let's entitle this post something like Being a "Lady" on Chemo. I have to come up with a better title and I will, but, in general, I just keep thinking about how difficult it is to be ladylike with all the side effects.*
>
> *Don't worry, I won't make this gross because, of course, that is not ladylike! :-) We know about the hair. Enough of that already, right? But, you know I am losing ALL hair - not just that on my head. The benefit of that is no more shaving my legs for a while.*
>
> *The downside of that is no more eyebrows. It is not very ladylike to walk around without eyebrows. (They are not totally gone yet on me, but they are headed that way.) Fortunately, God created make-up, and so I can try to do something about that.*
>
> *Oh, along with hair, fingernails change. Mine are peeling, and, of course, it is sooo unladylike to have chipped peeling fingernails! Thank heavens my manicurist comes to my house and will be here today!*
>
> *Years ago I started telling myself GCL. Instead of counting to 10 when things happened - when something was said - I would say GCL standing for Be a Gracious, Charming Lady Donna. Hopefully, I could catch my tongue and not offer too ugly a response. However, I think chemo is taking away a bit of the "lady" element, so I may have to prop up the whole gracious, charming piece if I can. :-)*
>
> *Anyhow, that is my ladylike philosophizing for the day.*
>
> *Take care everyone...*

treatment, though, as it is more difficult to remove, and you don't need the extra chemicals at this time. You also don't want to rub excessively, as not only is that damaging to the delicate skin of your eye, but it can also pull out or damage your eyelashes. Don't forget to purchase new non-fiber mascara, as mascaras are often carriers of germs, which you want to avoid at all costs. Also, to avoid infection, consider purchasing disposable mascara wands.

As you address your lips, your goal is to redefine them as they may appear sunken in, due to the steroids. A lip liner can help to re-contour your lips, adding some definition that may be currently hidden. As you use a lip liner, know that these tend to be higher in color stain and pigment but also paraffin, so your lips may feel drier. Draw your lip line in using a rosey, blush shade to bring out a refreshed look to your face. As you apply a lip line, try using a series of connected dots, rather than drawing one continuous line. Another tip is to focus on the center of your lips, not the corners, as that will provide a refreshed look that is easier to maintain through the day.

For most people, as they are going through treatment, a lipstick will be the best option. It goes on more quickly, does not need to be as precisely applied, and can be hydrating to the lips. Again, as you strive for a refreshed and revitalized look, opt for rose and blush shades for your lipstick.

Finish your refreshed and luminous look with a little blush. A sheer pink or peach will help to counter the sullen look of your skin. The little pop of color on your cheeks will give you more of the rosey glow you are trying to achieve.

If you have an interest in having a little glamor, your lips are the place to bring in the color. However, remember that with a deeper color comes a little bit more work as darker colors should be meticulously applied and retouched often.

Even if you go for brighter, high pigment glamour type colors, as you go through treatment avoid the dark shades. The darker colors will be more dramatic, but more aging and often result in a look that is tired and dark as opposed to fresh and vibrant.

Donna

Let's call today's post The Face of Cancer.... So, I have been thinking about this for a while, talking about it for a week or two, now brave enough to do it tonight.

The question is why post these. Well...there are a few reasons...so let me explain.

Point 1: People have shown up to help and have been a bit shocked by what they see. As we approach the holidays and more people stop by, I don't want you to be shocked. I am on chemo - and there is a very real look to that. (I do try to get the wig and make-up on before people show up, but I am not always successful!)

Point 2: People who see me out frequently say that I don't look sick. I joke that I put on a smile, my make-up, and a wig and that I am set for the day. There is an enormous amount of truth in that. I don't want people to see me as "sick", but perhaps I do need you to know what "tired" is like for me. :-)

Point 3: I have had many people ask why in the world I took my new job. To take a big job on top of the chemo - even the surgeon looked at me yesterday, rather stunned. But, because I work, I get up and I put on my smile, put on my make-up, grab a wig, and put my best foot forward. If I didn't have to go to work, it would be too easy to look in the mirror all day and see picture number 1. And that would just be depressing. I don't need that!

So, there is my explanation. The first is of me as I got up Saturday morning. No make-up, very pale, a few sores on my face from the chemo, and, oh yes, no hair. Picture number two, I have applied my make-up. Mind you, that is an exceptionally long task!! Many layers are needed to make my eyes pop and seem bright. Now I know why chemo takes your hair. It is to give you more time to get the necessary make-up on. :-) In picture 3 I have thrown on my wig, and I am off for a fun-filled day.

Here is hoping you can always start your day with a smile, but keep your make-up to a minimum! :-)

Love to all...

Eyelashes

Some people lose eyelashes; others do not. As always, it depends on your chemo and your body. In my case, the eyelashes completely fell out several months after I had finished my chemo, catching me by surprise. However, because they fell out after my treatments were finished, I was able to apply Latisse, a prescription product that stimulates eyelash growth and worked well for me. Within two weeks I had little eyelashes again.

At first, I could not figure out what to do when my eyelashes were all gone. Yes, fake lashes were a possibility if there was a big event. But, in the spirit of avoiding things that could possibly cause infection, I did not want to apply them consistently.

> **Donna**
>
> *Item 2 for the day: No one tells you that you continue to lose your eyelashes and eyebrows AFTER chemo as well! Now, that info would have been useful. But, no, here we are two months after my last chemo with eyelashes and eyebrows still falling out.*
>
> *One word to solve this issue.... Latisse. A facialist told me that people who had chemo and lost their eyelashes (and eyebrows) grew them back much faster with Latisse.*
>
> *I am just saying....should you ever have the need...it works!*
>
> *In the meantime....take care!*

Eyebrows

Yes, I lost my eyebrows as well. They started falling out after my first chemo treatment, and, well, it was not very ladylike. I had heard that I might lose them, and a friend quickly said I should get them tattooed on. I looked into it, but my doctors were completely against it.

When eyebrows are tattooed on, you basically create multiple pinpricks in your skin in order to apply the color. Those pinpricks do have to heal and scab, like any other trauma to the skin. So, the last thing you want to do when undergoing cancer is to intentionally damage your skin and potentially introduce a contaminant. On top of which, it takes about two weeks for the eyebrows to heal after they are tattooed. So, all and all, not something to do while you are going through treatments.

I stuck with the tried and true and drew my eyebrows in every morning. I also made sure my wig had long enough bangs to float around the eyebrow a little, hoping that made my lack of eyebrows less obvious.

Eyebrows do typically grow back. Mine grew back just like they had always been, blond and straight. The one thing I found, though, is that to this day, the eyebrow on the left grows much faster and with much more hair than the eyebrow on the right. My friends and I laugh that I have a little "bush" on the right side of my face. Nothing that can't be easily remedied with a good brow wax.

MANIS AND PEDIS

So, I just have to say it. I can't avoid it any longer. There is a risk that you may lose your fingernails during treatment. ARGHHH! I know, right?? To be fair, *I* did not lose my fingernails. And, was I ever thrilled. But, it does happen. The spirit of this book is to let you know things so that you are prepared. So, now I have told you.

Knowing that losing your nails is a possibility, your approach with your nails should be as conservative as possible. This is not the time to apply fake nails, to get tips, to use gels. This is the time to have simple, filed nails. A little nail color is okay, but layering on the glue or other adhesives that often damage even healthy nails is not a good idea. Anything that may damage your nail makes it all the more of a risk, that as your body struggles with your treatments, you could lose your nails altogether.

If you are a fan of manicures and pedicures, cancer does not mean you need to stop these little pleasures. However, do take great care! First of all, purchase your own Mani/Pedi grooming set, especially the clippers and cuticle pushers. Insist that your manicurist use only your tools, in order to minimize the risk of infection.

You might check to see if your manicurist will come to your house. Mine was very willing to do that. You can soak your feet in a bath tub. Or, little pedicure blow-up tubs are available for a few dollars at a beauty supply store. Blow it up, soak your tootsies, and relax in your favorite room while your manicurist does the rest.

While I was fortunate not to lose my nails, my nails have not been very strong or "good" even four years since diagnosis. I forewarn you here because, even if you keep your nails, it is fair to expect changes in them. Again, your treatments will effect your entire body. Once you are finished with your treatments, it is not as if your body magically becomes fine again. The damage from the treatments may stay with you awhile. One way I still see the damage is in the form of weak nails.

A Butterfly Emerges

My father, as I have mentioned, is an engineer. A smart man, with a great, dry sense of humor, he is not what you would call a "talker." While I wrote on my blog about everything going on, others frequently chimed in to comment, but not Dad. That wasn't his style.

Except one day. The day I posted the blog with the three pictures of my transformation. My father wrote:

> **Donna,**
>
> *When you sent us the "before" photo, I wonder what you were thinking of posting this on your Care Bridge site, but the transformation into the "Beauty" was like a butterfly emerging from the cocoon! Your description of why you felt you wanted to share this transformation with all your friends and family was compelling. You have handled this setback with a lot of courage and it makes me proud that you are my daughter!*
>
> *Love,*
>
> *Dad*

We all do what we need to do to be radiant as we go through our cancer journey. My father comparing me to a butterfly emerging from a cocoon was so important to me, in so many ways. Every day as I went through treatment, I would see if I could find that butterfly, and what color she might be.

So, I share Dad's note with you as well. Find your inner butterfly. Be the beauty you can, remembering that your beauty begins with a smile.

BEAUTIFULLY RADIANT: YOUR INNER BEAUTY

We have all heard of the importance of a positive attitude in fighting a disease. We have also always heard that it is what is on the inside that counts. That sentiment is so much about attitude as well. So, how do you find your own inner beauty? How do you find that positive attitude during a trying time? How can you be beautifully radiant when your physical body is hurting?

This chapter is about finding YOUR inner beauty. I can share mine. I can share what others found that allowed them to be positive, to beam from the inside out. But, your inner beauty is unique. Maintaining and sharing that spirit as you go through your cancer will go a long way in helping you to truly feel like the lady you are.

As with the rest of the chapters, I and some other women share some of the tools that worked for us. I found several broad paths that helped me find my inner radiance: faith, humor, and the spirit of others. In sharing these tools, we hope to give you a few things to consider so that you can be beautifully radiant, despite the cancer.

FAITH

Many of us believe there is a higher power, a

> **Donna**
>
> *Wishing everyone a Blessed and Merry Christmas! On this day when we celebrate the birth of Christ, I also remember the many births in my life this year....*
>
> - *The rebirth of so many wonderful friendships...*
>
> - *The birth of nieces and nephews so dear....*
>
> - *The birth of many new friends during this cancer challenge... (Chelsey, Kristina, Lisa, thank you again!!)*
>
> - *The birth of new opportunities.....*
>
> *While cancer has not been fun, it's true blessing is all of you!*
>
> *Much love and warmest wishes this lovely Christmas day!*

greater God. Regardless of what kind or whether or not you formally practice a religion, spirituality and faith can be foundational to finding your inner radiant self. I can only speak to that which I know. So, I share the role that my faith and spirituality played for me in living like a lady.

I am Catholic. I grew up Catholic, attended Catholic school, and try always to practice my faith. But, never did I feel closer to God than when I had cancer. It was so odd. Going through the cancer and the multiple surgeries, I could have intellectually made the case for being angry at and blaming God, but, this isn't what I felt. I was calm. I had inner peace. I had my faith, and never was it stronger.

They say you find God when you are silent. I know there is nothing harder for me in my everyday, non-cancer fighting life, than being silent and listening to God. I think part of why my faith was so strong during the cancer is that I was quiet. I had no choice. I was sick. And, I listened.

Donna

On this Sunday, when my heart aches for the people in Arizona [the shooting of Congresswoman Gabrielle Giffords and eight others on Jan. 8, 2011], I want to talk about prayer and faith.

First, prayer. You know what is interesting? Once something tragic happens – like cancer - a magical door opens that allows everyone to "safely" say that they are praying for you. I mean, we see that on this blog, right, with how many times people say I am in their prayers, etc. But, we sorta know each other here, so it is safe. But, beyond that, almost complete strangers when they find out that I have cancer, immediately open up about God and faith and prayers. Why is that?

For example, the young 20-something-year-old who delivers me pizza once in awhile from my favorite place, Ami's. A few months ago, I opened the door and had neglected to put my wig on. I apologized and he asked what was wrong. I said chemo for breast cancer. Right away he said of course that he was sorry, but that he would pray for me. He left, saying, "Really, I am going to pray for you as I drive to my next delivery."

Another example. I called a favorite retail store to order some make-up. Because I explained that I was really tired from being on chemo, they brought the purchase to my car when I got there. The saleswoman, a stranger to me, right away said she would add me to her prayer list and would keep me in her prayers.

I find it fascinating that once something tragic happens, everyone seems to open up about prayer. But, why do we wait until something happens? Why don't we pray for people just because? Is it that prayer and God are so personal, that we don't feel comfortable sharing our faith? Or, is it that so many people receive such personal support through God that when something happens to someone else, they want to share the source of their support? Maybe it is a little of both. I may never know, but I have found this thought-provoking. I bet 95 percent of the people who find out I have cancer say they will pray for me. In a world that can seem a bit of a mess, how wonderful to know that there are so many people leading a faith-filled life.

Speaking of faith, many people have asked me how I really can seem to be doing so well through this. And, really, I am fine. What you see here is truly how I am handling everything. I think it might be faith. I truly believe that there is a reason for everything and that God has a plan. I firmly believe that he is with me on this journey and that my smiles are a reflection of the calmness I feel because of him. I feel very secure because of this. I trust God and the plan he has for me. My faith helps me feel less concerned, upset, scared for this next surgery. In fact, you could say I am excited as it is another step in bringing me a bit closer to the rest of God's plan for me. And you know me - I am the curious type!

Maybe faith and prayer are really linked. Well, we know they are, but let me explain my perspective. If people open up and pray, talk about prayer, talk about faith, etc., when something bad happens, well, maybe that is part of why bad things happen: to force the dialogue. To give people the "safe zone" to share their faith. Haven't we done that a bit here?

Maybe if there is something we can take away from this journey together it is that we don't have to wait for bad things to pray for each other. Maybe we can share our faith and our prayers a little more openly, and maybe we can pray for each other... just because.

With that, many prayers for each of you tonight...just because!

One thing that struck me about faith is that as I quietly listened and sat with God, I started to see how many times he was right in the middle of the situation for me. Again, on a busy, non-cancer fighting day, I might miss the hand he has in my life. But, during the times I was quiet, as when I was going through the cancer, he

> **Donna**
>
> *You know the Lord works in mysterious ways, and I think I was a beneficiary of another little item this week. I supervise about 25 people at work, and they are spread all over the globe. Only about four work here in St. Louis.*
>
> *So, early in the week I was putting together travel plans to visit a team member in New Jersey in the coming week. I figured I should travel on off weeks from chemo. Days later I show up in Minneapolis only to learn that as a cost cutting measure we were not to do anymore travel (except to meet with customers). So, to the team I expressed great disappointment that I wouldn't be able to travel to meet with each of them in person. Inside, though, I was doing cartwheels! Travel can resume in January most likely, and by then I should be done with chemo.*

was there in a brilliant manner. There were so many little times when God was quickly answering a concern, a prayer. Sometimes, I didn't even know I was going to need to make the prayer.

During my cancer treatments, because I was quiet and listened, I also heard and saw God's role in my life. Because I was willing to share what was going on by writing and speaking with those I loved, I focused on these events in a new way that allowed me to recognize God's hand

> **Donna**
>
> *For the church-goers among us, I think you will appreciate this little update. You know that I am struggling with this whole hair issue. So, I decided to wear my wig to church this morning. Not that I had to yet – I've not lost that much hair – but, I thought I should start easing into the idea of constantly wearing a wig.*
>
> *So, at church I just prayed that God would give me the grace needed to handle my hair loss well. As we finished the last song, a lovely woman behind me tapped me on the shoulder and said how beautiful my outfit was and how lovely I looked! Then, as I made my way to the exit, Sally – she and I are often Eucharistic ministers together – told me she just loved my new haircut!*
>
> *I didn't expect God to answer my prayer so quickly! But, am I ever glad he did. A few compliments were just what I needed this morning!*

in them. Because I was able to recognize God's hand, I was calm. My spirit, therefore, was kind, not angry.

Now true, I still often asked, "Really, God? Really?" And when I was exceptionally serious, I would say, "You've got to be kidding me, God." I joked with people that when I fell and injured my leg a year earlier, God had given me a timeout. However, since I still had not learned the lesson - I was still doing too much, not being quiet enough with him - he gave me another and a bigger timeout: cancer.

In my head, I see him shaking his head with a little smile and thinking to himself, Oh my child, please listen to me for a moment. It was in the listening that I found his spirit and, ultimately, mine.

GRIEF AND LOSS

We lose thousands of people each year because of cancer. There is great grief from the loss of life due to cancer. I am not going to pretend to have the correct words for those going though such painful loss of life of one they hold dear. I know that there are many sources of support out there for you, and I share some of these on the website LivingLikeALady.com. But, right now, I want to talk to women who are living with cancer. As we live with cancer, either through our treatments or as we move beyond our treatments, we also experience enormous grief and loss.

From the time you are first diagnosed, you will experience a series of losses; I know I did. A strong faith can help you to deal with the losses and associated grief, but it will not shield you from them. Acknowledging the losses as they are happening and grieving for them, without letting them swamp your recovery, is the best approach, allowing others to help you when possible. There is an order, a process to loss and grief. It starts with change: the realization that something of significance has changed in your world and life, as you knew it, in some respect, will never be the same. An important step is identifying the loss, peeling back the onion to explore and understand the loss you are experiencing. Once you have begun to understand it, you can then begin to address it, accepting or even embracing the pain and sadness associated with it. There are several types of losses that can be profoundly experienced through a cancer journey.

Loss of Future

When you hear the diagnosis that you have cancer, one of the first things you think about may be the loss of part of your body, or even life, itself. A diagnosis of cancer makes that possibility suddenly very real. Along with it comes the fear of never seeing your children grow up, leaving your spouse, losing the dreams that you have. Suddenly, you may feel that you have lost any certainty about your future. Often, as a result, regret sets in… why did I put off living?

As I reference earlier in the book, I had severely damaged my leg in a freak accident, before I was even diagnosed with cancer. Learning at the time that I may struggle ever to walk again, I felt a profound loss of future. If I couldn't walk, how would I work? How would I live the life I knew? Because I went through a strong sense of loss about my future with my leg injury, that was not necessarily the loss I felt during the cancer. For some reason, I never questioned whether I would live or die with my cancer. It wasn't until I was well past my treatments that the significance of the cancer and the journey I had been on occurred to me.

Loss of Dignity/ Humanity

Often there is a fear of being treated as less than a human being as you undergo treatments. No matter how caring your medical team is, there are constant tests, physical exams, even experimental procedures, all of which remind you that you are a patient, and as a patient, you are vulnerable. You may feel a loss of privacy and even dignity. Often those with cancer are afraid of being defined by their cancer; they fear that they will

Donna

I was taking my niece Leah to get a manicure with me. We pulled up at the manicurist's shop and my phone rang. I looked at my sister, Karen, I think it is the doctor. I answered it, and the doctor said she had "bad news." I started repeating everything out loud so that Karen would know what was happening.

I have cancer she said. At the time she thought it was stage 2, and we didn't really know the size. Call the office tomorrow. Let's schedule an appointment and start talking about what we need to do. Karen's eyes were damp. Leah was so quiet. I remember thinking, well, it appears I have cancer - here we go.

The manicurist waved to us as we sat in the car with an odd look on her face - what were we doing??? I looked at Karen and said, well, we better go in. Karen got out of the car as did Leah. Only Leah and I were getting manicures. Karen was driving home to pick up Andy. We were meeting my friend Kathy for dinner. Karen gave me a hug. I wasn't processing yet; she was. I just knew that I hated being late - for anything. Yes, even if I had just heard I had cancer.

Leah and I went in and got manicures. We did something very normal in a very non-normal time! Karen picked us up, with my nephew Andy in tow, when we were done. I didn't know whether she had told Andy or not. I figured she must have, but I wasn't sure.

We picked up Kathy, who bounced in the car with a book for me. Oh good, I exclaimed, I will need more reading material. She gave me an odd look. Yes, apparently I have breast cancer, I replied. I think I will be doing a lot of reading.

And so the journey began....

become their illness. And if they are defined by cancer, then they fear that will diminish them as people, as the individual they are. I would offer to you that a significant reason for this book is that while your body and medicine take on the cancer "fight", you can be a radiant lady with great dignity as you take on this disease. You are worthy of honor and respect because of who you are as a person, something you do not lose because cancer is striking your physical body.

Loss of Self Worth

Often there is a loss of self worth that comes from the loss of being able to do some of the things you could do before. This may be especially true for those who define themselves by a particular role or relationship or a job that is changed by the cancer. They strive to be the world's best Mom, or they are their job. This role or job gave them purpose and meaning… now what are they?

For me, the deepest loss was my sense of self worth. For years, I had been a corporate executive known for brand building. I had strived to manage my reputation, my image in the corporate community, with great control. From the beginning, I was considering a double mastectomy. However, the physical loss for me from the cancer was not my greatest fear. My greatest fear at diagnosis was that I would now be defined differently. I would be defined by my cancer. I might no longer be known as the branding thought leader, the trusted and talented corporate

> **Ellen**
> *I believe that our words feed our spirit. So, I kept my words positive to keep my spirit bright.*

executive. I feared that everything I had worked for career wise could be lost. The very thing I had controlled and built well, my own personal brand, might be lost, and I could not do a thing about it.

Whenever I am faced with anything, I take action, I take whatever control I can. And, that is what I did when I faced this potential self worth loss. I was not going to allow cancer to define me; I would define me. Thus, for as many days as I could, I got up, went to work, and lived a very "normal" life in a very non-normal situation. I took control of the things I could control, and that allowed me to work through the loss and grief I was experiencing. Along the way, I realized that the gifts God had given me could be used for quite a bit more than just building brands.

Every time I wrote in my blog about something I discovered, I was taking control of the situation. But, importantly, I also learned, I was sharing information that others valued. I realized that as I was searching for answers to living through my cancer and its treatments, that others needed that information as well. So, my processing of my loss was very much an accumulation of data, of facts, of information that would allow me to be a lady, despite everything swirling around me.

The processing of loss and grief are critical as you go through your cancer journey.

> **Kathy**
> *I sometimes thought that my cancers were a reminder that I don't have control over every aspect of my life. I was also very aware of the many, many people who were praying for me, and I attribute my sense of wellbeing to their support. I often said during the experience that I could "feel" the prayers. It's hard to describe.*

If you don't identify them, if you don't explore them but simply shove them away, they will come back to haunt you. If you try to push through it…try to stuff it…try to ignore it… and don't deal with it, the loss gets "parked," and it remains in that "parking lot" until you deal with it.

How to deal with these losses, this grief? Consider your spiritual journey. I, and many women I talked to, surprisingly experienced calmness in their cancer journey because of faith. Faith and spirit reminded me that losing my breasts was not the end; it was simply a step to my future. Faith stabilized me because through it I knew there was something far greater than the physical challenges. Faith also helped me look for the little bits of grace each day. Knowing that God was with me, I could smile or have a kind word even if physically I was in pain. Importantly, faith allowed me to let go, to recognize that

I was not in control. I chose to trust God. I chose to live and to try to live radiantly, despite my physical changes, but that choice hinged strongly on my faith that God has a plan for me and would take care of me. If you rely on your faith and mourn the losses along the way that really matter to you, you will find a sense of peace, a calmness that opens your heart to the possibilities of life.

While the loss and grief of cancer are real for you, they are also very real for those you love. They especially feel such a lack of control. You have a choice on how you handle your cancer, the attitude you take, the spirit with which you live, the doctors you find to battle your disease. Family and friends, on the other hand, feel like they can only do little more than watch, and experience great loss as well as they recognize a significant change in you and, therefore, their lives. There are resources for your family and friends as well as they travel this cancer journey with you. I encourage you to encourage them to look for caregiver support. The cancer journey will strongly impact you and those who love you.

Everyone's journey with cancer is different. In a spiritual sense, I imagine everyone carrying a cross, and that the cross is different for each person. Each person is carrying the cross at a different height, some are weighted down, others are standing tall, others fall and get back up. We can't compare cancers, or approaches, or severity because we cannot compare lives. We have each had unique experiences that have helped to form us. As such, our journeys through cancer are unique. As you travel your own journey, recognize the loss you are facing and work through your grief. Don't compare yourself to someone else. Don't say that this is not as bad as such and such. This is your journey, your cancer, and your cancer journey is significant.

HUMOR

I laughed a lot during my cancer. I tried to find humor every step of the way. For one, it made it easier for me to deal with an issue. But, importantly, if I was laughing, it was easier for others to deal with something as well.

> **Donna**
> From my perspective - Floppy (the name for my injured leg) has a mind of its own and is jealous of all the attention Lumpy has been getting. However, for statements like this, you all may just call me "Dopey"! :-)

To begin with, I named my offending body parts. Okay, I know that sounds really quite weird, but, I did not want to be defined by cancer. Likewise, I did not want damaged body parts to define me, either. So, I had "Lumpy" and "Lumpy Lite." Lumpy, of course, was the breast with cancer, and lumpy lite was the other side.

The other thing with naming the body parts is that it made it much easier for me to discuss this journey with others. As you go through your treatments, stuff will happen. I didn't want to have to say my "left breast" or "cancer" every other sentence. I wanted to be able to share some of the things happening, in a non-threatening way.

To an extent, I realized the importance of this on the day I discovered I had cancer. My sister, young niece, teenage nephew, and a friend headed out to dinner. Everyone knew that I had just learned that I had cancer, but no one was talking about it at dinner.

> **Jackie**
> I had a mastectomy and did not have reconstruction. I had been married for a few years when the cancer struck. I just didn't know how my husband would react to my appearance post surgery. When I finally felt brave enough to show him, Bud looked at me, smiled, and said, "It looks like you are winking at me."

Finally, my nephew piped up with, "If no one will say the word cancer, can we at least all say that Aunt Donna has an illness in her breast?" We all burst out laughing, and we still do when one of us retells that story. Yes, we can say I have an illness in my breast. The important thing was to figure out how to talk about it.

Not everyone is comfortable laughing during cancer. Some friends couldn't believe that I was finding things humorous. But, others knew that for me, it was a comfortable way of handling it. In a very real way, I was trying to take care of my friends and family. They were looking at me and seeing the face of cancer, and to help them, I wanted to lighten the load and felt that humor could do that a bit.

Another point on all of this is that some of the things that will happen to you, will happen regardless of how you approach things. Choosing to smile is empowering and gives you an ability to spell your cancer with a small c.

Ultimately, your use of humor is where your unique spirit comes out. If that is not you, don't force it. If it is you, don't be afraid of it. To be your radiant self, you simply need to let who you are come out as genuinely as possible.

THE SPIRIT OF OTHERS

For some reason, as I went through my cancer, I saw others in my life so much more clearly. Importantly, I met new people, some as a result of having cancer and others in day-to-day life, with almost a sense of awe. Perhaps I was listening better. Perhaps I was more curious. Perhaps it was just great not to focus on myself. Regardless of the genesis, people said things and stood out in ways that I had not recognized before.

Really seeing the spirit of others encouraged me to find a positive spirit for myself. Just when you are so sick that you do not know how you will stand up that day, you meet a special person, a gift, who helps you to see how lovely people can truly be.

Donna

On this Palm Sunday, I want to share the story of Mary. I wanted to write it Thursday when I met her, I just didn't have the energy, and I wanted to give Mary the story she deserves. You see, on Thursday I was back at infusion - getting my "little" chemo or Herceptin. At the end of my aisle was this tiny woman, telling one story after another. We all heard, and she was a delight. So she told the story of her dog three times straight; she is sick. We all are.

At one point, she got up to go to the restroom and walked right by me. As thin as a rail, with a hat on to hide her baldness, and no teeth, she used a walker while the nurse pushed her IV tubes along. As she left the restroom, Mary was dragging the walker with her - not using it - declaring loudly that she would much rather dance with her IV pole. When she passed by I said to her, "You are someone I must meet!" And, I meant it. A little later, after her infusion bags were changed, I heard her ask a nurse if she could come down and visit with me. The nurse said of course; she wants to meet you, too.

So, Mary came on down, leaving her walker behind, and plopped down next to me. She asked about my e-reader (iPad), and we hit it off instantly. Later, she admitted that the e-reader was just an excuse to talk to me and to start the conversation. Mary is 53. To look at her you would think she is closer to 83. This is her seventh brain tumor, although when they found this last one seven weeks ago, they also found lung cancer.

Mary told me she has six months to live. And living she will do. She called her children in Texas to see if she could stay with them these next several months. Of course they said yes, but she explained that they just don't understand. This will be so hard on them. Much harder on them than it will be on her.

In this our first meeting, we talked about everything: living, dying. God, heaven, what matters, what doesn't. She is not afraid of dying, by the way. Pretty much she can't wait to get to heaven she said, to get a "good spot" for her family! She just knows she will have her 30 year old body back, and her only fear is that her friends and family won't recognize her up there. The one thing that bothers her is that now that people know she is dying, they are coming out of the woodwork to tell her how much she has mattered to them. They remember the tiniest little thing that she did that so touched them, the kind word she said, the smile she shared. She said to me, if I have one piece of advice, don't wait until someone is dying to let them know how much they meant to you, to say thank you to them. Tell them while they are in the midst of living. It will matter so much to them, and maybe then they can do it even more. I thought that was awesome advice. She wanted me to pass the word on-and so I do.

Mary asked for my email address. We are going to be email pals while she is in Texas. What a special person - to want to build new friendships while she goes through this process of dying. Which brings me back to Palm Sunday. Our Pastor spoke of Palm Sunday and Holy Week as the journey. That life - what we learn, what we do, what is special - is because of this journey we take. What a journey Mary is on. Yet, bringing people into her fold is more important than ever as she sees her last few months. I am sharing Mary's message and love of life with you...so we can all take it forward. So we can all remember to thank someone sincerely, love someone out loud, and appreciate everyone. Perhaps now, a little of Mary's journey can be intertwined with all of ours.

With love and blessings to each of you...

ATTITUDE

As discussed in earlier chapters, attitude is so important in dealing with cancer. The question is, what is the genesis of your positive attitude? Some mornings I could not wake up and just say, "Ok, I will be positive today." It took more than that. My attitude had to come from some other place. It came from my faith, without a doubt. It came from my willingness to laugh, when many things were anything but funny. It came from seeing the unique special spirit of others that I met.

I learned that being a lady through cancer is very much about the attitude I took through my journey. I realized that my inner beauty came from

> **Kathy**
>
> *I believe a positive attitude has a lot to do with my outcome, so I worked on that. Of course, having been blessed with early detection for both cancers made having a positive attitude easier! I also thought through the few decisions I was given to make. I did research on each of my cancers because knowing what was happening enabled me to feel some level of control while having a disease that was out of my control. Making deliberate decisions helped me regain some of that control.*

my attitude, and my attitude was a reflection of my faith. I used humor to help others talk about some difficult topics. I found that spirit for myself. I found my radiant spirit through this cancer journey.

My question for you is what is your attitude? What is the source of that attitude? Importantly, can you use this time to rely on the faith you might have to find your inner beauty? Does humor play a role for you? Are there people you are meeting along the way that you want to get to know? What can help you shine despite the ravages to your body?

> **Donna**
>
> *With that I will leave you with a lovely comment made by the main attending physician at the hospital this week. As he prepared to leave from one of his visits, he said to me, "We need to get you well; the world needs you."*
>
> *What an AWESOME thing to say! He may say it to every single patient - and that is absolutely perfect. It's a very empowering statement. And for whoever reads this blog now or as a book someday, know that the world needs you!*

SUPPORT

CHOOSING YOUR CARE PROVIDERS

You learn you have cancer, and you realize you need to find a doctor, someone who specializes in cancer. Wow! Whom to call? It seems like this should be easy. But, finding the right doctor for you, for your situation, in your recovery process, you may not even know what types of doctors you need to find. So, let's discuss this and provide you with some tools for finding your medical team.

The most important thing to remember is that this is your body. You need the doctors, the specialists, the team that is best for you!

Types Of Doctors

Among the doctors you may need are specialists in the oncology arena, including a medical oncologist, a radiation oncologist, and an oncologic surgeon. Depending on your cancer, there may be other doctors needed as well, such as a plastic surgeon.

Medical Oncologist: Will typically manage your overall care and coordinate your chemo, medications, and other medical aspects of your treatment. Typically, he or she will closely watch your blood, side effects, and other indicators to determine how your body is managing the treatment and whether the treatment is working on the cancer.

Radiation Oncologist: A specialist in providing targeted radiation for the treatment of cancer. You may or may not need radiation, and if you do not, you will not need the radiation oncologist. An initial visit with a radiation oncologist will determine if radiation treatments will be helpful to you. Should you have to go through radiation, this doctor will ensure you are receiving the correct doses in the correct location.

Oncologic Surgeon: A specialist in the removal of cancer, whose expertise is often localized, such as a breast oncologist surgeon or a colorectal surgeon.

Plastic Surgeon: Should you be addressing breast, head, or neck cancer, a plastic surgeon with an expertise in reconstruction will be an important member of the team. He or she will work closely with your cancer team in an effort to restore your physical form and beauty.

These three oncology doctors make up your core cancer medical team, discussing with you your treatment, determining the approach, and deciding the order of treatments. There is an enormous advantage to having all of your doctors at one hospital or in one system as it makes it easier for them to talk with each other and develop your treatment plan as well as access your medical records, including having a common electronic medical record.

However, do not feel that all your doctors have to be

> **Judy**
>
> *I was blessed to have a great support system: my team of doctors - the pusher (my chemo doc), the zapper (my radiologist), my surgeon (Dr. P) - and their team of nurses. Along with my breast specialist that gave me what us girls called a fluff after my lumpectomy and moved tissue around in my breast so you could no longer see the dent that took the place of my missing tissue/tumor. They had the same sense of humor as I did. This was VERY IMPORTANT! And they allowed me to ask any and all questions. I had a lot of them. Everyone needs to have faith and trust in their doctor(s). This will help keep you as relaxed as possible and to continue to live your life and heal.*

at the same hospital or in the same hospital system. If you find a medical oncologist you like at one hospital system and a surgeon you prefer at another, that is completely your prerogative. In this case, though, you may have to do more of the coordinating with them at a time you are fatigued and not feeling well. However, what is most important is that you are comfortable with and trust the team that is taking care of you.

FINDING YOUR TEAM

So, how do you find the best doctor for you?

To start with, the doctor who has diagnosed you will likely make a referral. If you are being diagnosed through your general practitioner's office, they will probably have someone they typically refer patients to. Very often a first referral is to a surgeon. This is typically done because a biopsy is required to confirm a diagnosis.

Your referring physician will likely send you to the oncology surgeon or medical oncologist in his or her own hospital system; however, again, do not feel that you must stay in that hospital system. You may have a great doctor, in a wonderful hospital system, but there may be better cancer treatment in another system or facility. This is not the time to be super loyal to particular doctors or hospital. This is the time to be selfish and find out what is best for you!

A very important piece of identifying the right team of doctors is personality types and fit with you, the patient. Find doctors that you feel you connect with personally. These people will be on a long journey with you, and you want to trust and feel comfortable with them.

While you are looking for the experts that you connect with personally, you also have to consider your insurance plan and what that will cover. If a provider is "out of network," identify the additional costs you may have. Often, the doctor offices, themselves, can be the best source of some of this information.

ADDITIONAL TEAM MEMBERS

So, you have your medical oncologist, your oncologic surgeon, and perhaps a radiation oncologist. Hopefully, that is all you will need. But, it might not be as well. For instance, if you have breast cancer and end up needing a mastectomy or double mastectomy, you may also want to proceed with breast reconstruction. That surgery will be done by a plastic surgeon. So as you go through your treatment plan, you will need to find that doctor.

Another consideration is the particular side effects you experience and what type of specialist is best at addressing those. In my case, some significant lung side effects caused me to have to find a pulmonologist or lung specialist. Some side effects can be managed by medications, but you may also find relief through alternative modalities, such as acupuncture for fatigue, neuropathy, or nausea or a healing touch massage for pain relief. If alternative modalities are of interest to you, make sure to work with your oncology team so that they can support you with these efforts.

Again, the same recommendations exist. As you go through your treatments and discover another specialist is needed, find the one that is best for you. The doctors will talk to each other, and your core team will have some good referrals for you along the way.

RECOMMENDATIONS

It goes without saying that recommendations will be a great way to find the right cancer team for you. Close friends or family members that have dealt with cancer are another good source of recommendations.

This is also the time to reach out to any doctors and nurses you know, even casually, to ask for a recommendation. The medical community, like so many communities, is tightknit. And, the doctors will know who in their community are considered exceptional. If you don't have friends in the medical arena, ask your primary care or another doctor you have seen before to ask his or her advice.

I received the referral to my eventual surgical oncologist from my orthopedist. As soon as he heard about my cancer diagnosis, he made a call to ensure I was seen by who he knew to be one of the best in the area. She was wonderful and a perfect fit for me. Before long, my team was being put into place. I did choose to have all my cancer doctors in one center, as I wanted them to be able to easily discuss the approach to my treatment.

YES, INTERVIEW THE DOCTORS

Everything feels very surreal when you find out you have cancer. Things start moving quickly as you go from medical appointment to medical appointment. Bringing along a friend or a family member, especially to the early appointments can be really helpful. My friends who went with me would comment afterwards that while I was calmly asking questions, my hands were always shaking. No matter how nervous you feel, though, take the time to ask the questions, truly interview the doctors. It's your life, after all. Not only do you want to find out how they plan on treating you, you want to find out how you will work with them in the process.

Keep a journal through this process. Write down your questions and the answers you receive. Sort through your information that way and insert new questions, as they occur to you. What type of questions? There are so many, but a few to start with include:

- What is the specific type of cancer I have?
- What type of treatment protocol do you recommend for the type of cancer I have?
- How frequently have you treated what I have? What are your typical outcomes for this?
- What can I as a patient do to achieve the best result possible?
- How long should I expect to be in treatment?

The first radiation oncologist I met with was considered to be outstanding in her field, but I found her very arrogant. I was frustrated that she kept stopping me and telling me she did not need to hear what was going on with me. Given all the complications I had, I sure as heck thought she had better listen to me. Don't be afraid to find someone different if the "chemistry" is not there, if you find yourself not trusting or respecting the doctor. You will end up having a long relationship with these people, so you want the fit to be a good one. Keep in mind that your comfort with your doctors and their abilities will help you feel more comfortable overall and less stressed, which, in turn, improves outcomes.

Do not be afraid of taking the time of talking to a number of doctors. While you want to move quickly, it is critical that you get the right team for you. So, get second and third opinions. Consider their bedside manner, their knowledge, their experience in treating YOUR type of cancer. Consider their environment: a great doctor in a depressing environment may not be the overall best solution for you. It is common in medicine that patients get multiple opinions and make decisions for one doctor or another for a variety of reasons. This isn't about hurting their feelings; it is about getting rid of your cancer.

> **Donna**
>
> *Because there are two main tumors, the surgeon wants to see if the smaller one is gone due to the chemo. If so, we may be able to do the lumpectomy. The type of surgery will help influence when I have the surgery as well.*
>
> *Secondly, the surgeon will speak to the radiation oncologist so we can see whether radiation will be needed or not. The surgeon is concerned that because my cancer was stage 3, and because of the size, I may need radiation regardless.*
>
> *Finally, they are setting me up with a plastic surgeon. Often they do the first part of the reconstruction at the same time that they do the mastectomy. But there are all sorts of limitations, doing radiation before reconstruction but post mastectomy. You must be off chemo a certain number of weeks before reconstruction, etc., etc.*
>
> *The net of all this is, if you think God laughs when we plan, you should have heard the doctors! ☺*
>
> *The doctors all need to talk and then they will decide what course to take. I trust them, and they are outstanding. It is just this little "control" issue I have that is troublesome.*

EVERYONE LOVES HER OWN DOCTOR

As you continue on your cancer journey, you will meet many others who have cancer or who know people who have had cancer. One thing you will quickly learn is that everyone LOVES her own doctor. And, rightly so. Her doctor got rid of her cancer, allowed her to move on with her life.

The challenge is that many times, people will try to tell you that you MUST go to their doctor, to their hospital or cancer center. In the beginning, when you are just getting your team together, this pressure can be daunting. Are you getting the right team? Are you going to the right place? Know this: You need to do what is right for you. Just because a particular place or team was right for someone else does not make your team wrong. This is not the time to second guess yourself. If you have found doctors you trust with a system you respect, be comfortable and confident in that decision as it is right for you.

People may sound like they are questioning your decision. They are not trying to be rude. They want you to have the medical success they have had. Be calm, be confident, and firmly tell them that you are pleased they had such great success, and you trust that your team will do the same for you.

THE REST OF YOUR DOCTORS

I'll never forget going to my orthopedic surgeon, who had been treating my unrelated broken leg, just a few days after my diagnosis. He walked in the room and said, "The heck with your leg; let's talk about your breast." That was so important for me to hear as I began to understand that the cancer was what mattered to all of my care providers.

I learned very early that you need to share absolutely everything with every one of your care providers. You can also certainly ask your oncology team to forward your medical records to every doctor you see from your GP to your OB-GYN

> **Donna**
>
> *So, yesterday at the orthopedist, they also took x-rays of my leg again. Then they began the discussion of how people can live without ACLs - with enough cartilage and strong quad muscles. See, the problem is, I heard this entire discussion a year and a half ago. We learned the hard way that, in fact, I do need an ACL. (Ankle fracture and tendon tears anyone?)*
>
> *So, what to do? First of all, we don't know exactly what the problem is with the reconstructed knee/ACL. Could be weak, torn, damaged, who knows. We did know that knee problems were possible once I began treatments for the cancer, at least my orthopedic surgeon was concerned.*
>
> *You see my ACL was rebuilt using a cadaver tendon and pins. Chemo tries to destroy anything foreign in your body, so it is highly likely that chemo tried to destroy the tendon. On top of which, the tendon had only been in me for eight months when chemo started. Anyhow, until we do an MRI, we won't truly understand the extent of the damage. Meanwhile, I will do PT to strengthen my quad and keep wearing my brace.*

to your orthopedic surgeon and everyone in between.

Each doctor will have different things that will matter to him or her. So, sharing more rather than less will only prove helpful. Let them decide what not to read. For example, my OB was very concerned with the type of cancer, as that helped him to know where cancer could potentially migrate to in the future for me. My orthopedic surgeon was concerned with the chemo and the impact it might have on my newly reconstructed knee.

Your Care, Post Cancer

Once you have had cancer, there are definitely new considerations with your medical team! Understand that you may very well be seeing your medical oncologist for years. Once the primary cancer treatments have stopped, it may be every three months. After a few years, every six months you will follow up. Before too long, usually around five years post cancer, you will see the medical oncologist about once a year. He or she will always draw blood as looking for those cancer markers and other indicators of something going awry is the best way of catching it early.

You may very well stop seeing your surgical oncologist first, as long as she or he knows you are in good hands with a medical oncologist and you have healed well. You may gradually reduce the visits to the radiation oncologist to once a year as well.

Seeing your medical team does not excuse you from seeing your other care providers! In fact, you should be more diligent than ever as they also monitor you for potential additional cancers.

You are 10 years out post cancer, come down with the flu, and head to Urgent Care. Make sure to tell the doctor that you had cancer! I know it has been 10 years, but you had the cancer, it impacted your body, and you need to let medical care providers know this. It may effect what they consider or look for, even when you think it is simply the flu.

Fundamentally, think of the doctors as your team. Find the people you trust. Share the information about you and your cancer as much as possible. Do what is right for you and your body. And know that in your new normal, many of them have an important and constant part in your life moving forward.

THE GIRLS WILL GATHER

I didn't fully understand the power of the girls. I knew intellectually of "girl power" and what women were so capable of achieving. But, I didn't understand deep in my soul, what women can do when called.

> **Donna**
> *What a wonderful evening I had last night!! Two dear friends, Patty and Deborah, put together a lovely cocktail party with some amazing women. Between a little wine, a beautiful evening, and these wonderful women, it was a great night!*

This little get-together was an interesting introduction for me into the concept that the girls will gather. These two friends organized a group of six to eight women to come to my house. The purpose - to figure out how they all could help me. To put together plans, to identify jobs, roles, needs, you name it.

The challenge - I just didn't know what I would need. Ultimately, what was important was knowing they were there. And, truly, a slight turn of phrase in my blog, a tired voice on the phone, it didn't take much for the women to come out and take care.

I did need much support during my cancer journey. I found that during treatments and doctor visits, the support took two different paths. Sometimes people joined me, there to hear what was being said as I just couldn't take in all of the various

> **Donna**
> *The highlight of the day was my good friend Jennifer stopping by, bringing me a bit of lunch and us talking and laughing awhile. Almost forgot about all this "crud" my system is fighting with Jen here!*

information. I also learned early on that having an objective set of ears was critical. Friends would hear things differently than I would, they could help me with decisions, they would bring different views to the situation.

When I first found out I had cancer, friends as well as a tape recorder tracked everything a doctor said so that we could compare notes, and they could help me make informed decisions. Often we planned that after an appointment we would go out for a bite or a drink, just so we could confer on what had just been said.

I always had someone with me at chemo; it just seemed very important. Granted, sometimes these very dear friends would be running, getting lunch for us or something from the pharmacy.

Often, the most important role was simply to keep me company. There wasn't as much information to take in during chemo. There were just lots of drugs flowing into me, and so a friend at my side was wonderful. I never slept through chemo; often I tried to work. I tried not to wear the mantle of sick, but the mantle of Donna, corporate executive, friend, anything but cancer patient.

My mother was in town and went to my second chemo with me. My chemos lasted anywhere from five to seven hours long. After a few hours when

> **Donna**
>
> *The highlight of today was the support of dear friends. Deborah - what a dear you are! She left work to take me to the appointment, and then we went out for lunch and a bit of girl talk. What a positive and spirited friend! Quite the inspiration.*
>
> *My friend Liz from up the street had seen me in the morning, and hearing that I had an ankle procedure on top of my chemo going on today, offered to bring dinner by tonight. It was wonderful! While she is taking care of a lovely family - six and two year old daughters - she still had time to take care of me as well. Liz - thank you!*
>
> *You know many of you call or write to me directly or through this blog and share how much you appreciate hearing about how I am doing.*
>
> *I have to say, all of you are my inspiration! To have so many friends, far and near, caring, concerned, and offering support has really touched me. And for that, I thank you!*

she realized all was fine with me, she started visiting all of the other chemo patients. I just had to laugh, as this was so like her! Many patients didn't have company, and she hated to see that for them. To both of us, chemo just doesn't seem like something you should go through alone. Of course, I had to give her grief for leaving my side. She knew I was handling it well, given that I could also needle her.

PLANNING

In order to help me through treatment, many friends asked for a plan. The idea was to put everything on a schedule and then people could take turns. We learned that five days after my chemo is when I would feel the worst, so some people wanted to sign up for soup duty. Others wanted to be on the list to take me to appointments. Still others wanted to know when they should stop by and bring lunch or dinner, or just visit.

What we didn't understand about cancer is that you cannot plan very well. The only thing we now know with any certainty is that there is no certainty. A surgical complication from the mastectomy kept me in the hospital longer. My body struggling with the chemo drugs caused my chemo to be delayed a few times.

My family is spread all over the country, so they had plane tickets to buy if they were going to come to help out. For a family of planners, the uncertainty of chemo posed a challenge. However, the entire family learned to relax a little and just take each day as it came. If they had bought a ticket and chemo was changed, they would just help with whatever needed to be done at that time, in that moment.

All that being said, we did try to put together a schedule. As much as anything, trying to control the situation in a little way was important.

We marked potential chemo days, doctor visits, when I might be sick from chemo days, when meals might be needed, and sent it around to people. Family chose first, and then friends filled in. Minimally, I knew whom to call if there was a change in plans.

Things To Do

What can friends and family do? That is the question that is often posed. However, for me, the question was what would I allow them to do. You see, I am independent and am used to handling things on my own.

I had to learn that my gift to my friends and family was allowing them to help, that this didn't diminish me, but, rather, gave them a chance to express their care and love to me. That was an important lesson for me to learn.

So, what can you do for a friend going through cancer? There actually are many

> **Donna**
>
> Hello Dear Family and Friends....
>
> I do hope this finds everyone well and enjoying their weekend! Let me start by saying it is one of those dreaded Sundays because I know chemo occurs again tomorrow. Sighhhh.... For this chemo my family is not coming to town. But, not to worry. I have some of the world's best friends right here in St. Louis, and different people have "signed" up to help out on different days. Dear Patty will take me to chemo tomorrow. Many others are planning on stopping by, bringing me soup, and just generally checking up to make sure I am getting through the week all right.

things. First of all, consider this. Don't just ask a family member or friend going through cancer what she needs. If you see something small that needs doing, just take care of it. As soon as you ask, you have shifted the burden to the cancer patient, herself. The things that often mean the most are those that you as a friend or family member just see and do. Putting dishes away, sweeping up the floor, wiping down the bathroom. Even the basics are tiring when you are going through treatment, so someone just taking care of a "little" item can be huge.

Beyond just stepping in unasked on small tasks, there are other helpful things you can do once you have an understanding of what is needed. Many times, talking to a family member or close friend can provide the ideas you need to be supportive. Some suggestions that many women shared with me to be helpful include:

Food: The first thing to consider when buying food is that the chemo patient's sense of taste may have significantly changed. So ask her what sounds good, what she can eat, or more importantly, what she *will* eat. People brought soups that had a spice to them (knowing how much I love spice), but I ended up not being able to eat them at the time, as I just couldn't tolerate the spices. Fixing something that your friend already has in the house and is eating is another great option.

Also, consider running to the grocery store. The few times I headed to the store myself, I could maybe walk one or two aisles

> **Donna**
>
> *Happy Halloween Everyone!*
>
> *Before I retire for the night - a special call-out to my dear friends Steph and Jenn who came by for a few hours yesterday to clean my closets. By the time they pulled out all the winter clothes and shoes and put away the summer items, I was exhausted - from watching them, of course! ☺ They wouldn't let me raise a finger.*
>
> *How special it is to have friends who just step in and do everything – from bringing soup, to running to the store, to taking me to chemo, to cleaning my closets. Am I ever lucky!*
>
> *Here is hoping that the blood counts are better and that the chemo is a go tomorrow.*
>
> *Happy Halloween and lots of love to all...*

before I was too tired and had to sit and rest. On days I felt better, I might go to the store with someone and rest while she collected the items on my list. Other times, friends would get my list and run to the store on my behalf. That was so helpful.

Appointments: Offer to take your loved one to appointments, from doctor appointments to lab and x-ray to fun things like a manicure. Sometimes, just the driving and the appointment, itself, can be exhausting, even if it is something "fun." So, knowing that you don't have to drive, that someone is taking care of that, is a great relief.

Errands: Even though someone is in treatment, she still has errands to do. From picking up dry cleaning to getting the children to soccer games to running to the post office, the errands never stop. Running a few errands is a wonderful thing to offer a lady who is fatigued from treatment. To you it might be an errand; to her, it is rest and no worry, while providing a checkmark on the "To Do" list.

Cleaning and Organizing: In addition to doing little things while you

---

Donna

I started to see such a special side of life. The friends, the love, the support.

Mary Beth came by with lunch, and I am sure she can well attest to the fact that I had at best my "d" game going. I could hardly string three words together. :-)

Kathy came by with some dinner for me that night. She even called Mom and Dad to report in as I didn't think my fingers had the strength to dial the phone.

Saturday I woke up feeling better, and the friends kept pouring in!! Jackie with breakfast, Deborah with lunch, Angela with additional sustenance. And those who didn't stop by called. Always with the same reminders to eat and to drink my water!

So I am a "published author" at a loss for words. How do I possibly thank everyone? How do I express the love and caring I felt through this time from everyone? I am in awe of the wonderful people in my life and the kindness they showered on me.

So, yes, it was truly a special weekend. Not because I was sick from the chemo, but because of all the lovely people in my life who moved that Mack Truck out of the way.

God bless you all!

Donna

are visiting, more involved cleaning can be a great help. Cleaning is a big deal. Remember, as someone goes through treatment, she may be quite sick, and her immune system is compromised. So, cleaning a room, really disinfecting a bathroom, for instance, is an outstanding offer of support.

Having someone help me to organize was also a big help. As my treatments went from summer to winter, I needed to dig out my warm clothes. I really did not have the energy to move clothes around, so friends coming over to rearrange was an enormous gift.

Just Being: Sometimes the most wonderful thing you can do for a loved one going through cancer is just to be there with him or her. You can talk about the cancer. Or, you don't have to. You can talk the politics of the day, the children, the weather, whatever seems to work. The important part is often simply the companionship. More than one person, upon learning I was working on this book, told me I should include a list of what to say and what not to say to someone with cancer. I don't know that I could ever come up with a good or correct list, because it so depends on the person. My perspective is, be a friend by listening, looking for clues as to what your loved one going through treatment wants to talk about. I often wanted to hear about anything that would make me smile. I would talk about the cancer, if I felt it helped my friend, but, I got tired of talking about this cancer thing and me. I wanted to focus on other topics instead.

All that being said, when visiting with a friend or loved one, be very careful with the time. Know that the lady who can typically talk for hours may be exhausted after 30 minutes, and she may not want to tell you. I was always so appreciative of those visiting with me that I would never dream of telling them I had to rest. I didn't want them to take it the wrong way!

Surprise Visits: Not everyone loves surprise visits when they are going through cancer treatment. While the intention is wonderful, many ladies like to be prepared in some way, shape, or form for company. Be it to straighten up the home, put on a wig, maybe simply apply some lipstick, they may want to do what they can to "host" a friend. When they are going through treatment, they may be so fatigued that the house is a little messier than usual or they may be napping or too tired even to answer the door. To that end, before you start calling on a lady in treatment, check with her to see if unexpected visits will be welcomed or not.

HELP IS HEALING

In allowing people to help, to be there for me, I experienced the

> ### Donna
>
> *We had book club tonight. I LOVE book club. Let me explain... About six years ago Mary Beth and I were talking. We are both spiritual, and we would often discuss the challenges of having a "big" job while trying to live a spiritual and grace-filled life. We knew we weren't the only women with this challenge; we knew friends who struggled with it, too. So, we decided to start a book club. There are just six of us. We read a faith-based book, a spiritual book, and share what we are learning and how it applies to our life in our discussions. This is a "no-skip" meeting for me.*
>
> *I always leave this group of women so inspired, so touched, so amazed at how they live their lives. And tonight was no different. We have been through a lot together: death in a family, illness, a new baby (how is Gracie two already?), job woes and more job woes, concern over family, children growing up, and now breast cancer.*
>
> *And always we share, we learn, we support, and we look for the spiritual guidance to handle things with kindness and grace. Tonight, we didn't quite get to our book. That happens sometimes. But, we talked about cancer, my journey and the journey others are on as well. And what a beautiful night it was.*
>
> *Thank you dear book club friends for your support, your love, and for helping me stay on a beautiful spiritual path.*
>
> *You are all a blessing to me....*
>
> *With love to all*

love and care of my friends. Those very friends that I want to shower with love showered me right back.

During my cancer journey, I tried to stay true to the pieces of my life that really mattered before cancer struck. Book club is one of those important elements. I knew I needed this special group of women more now than ever before. Maureen knew how much this group meant to me (to her, to all of us), so she would pick me up and take each month. She was concerned that even if I had the energy to drive there myself, I wouldn't have the energy to drive home safely. Of course, I always argued with her, protesting that I could drive, but, of course, she was right. I live in the opposite direction of most of my book club friends, so, dear Maureen would add an hour or so to her evening out.

One particular book club meeting was especially meaningful. Everyone had been following my journey through my Caring Bridge blog, but, we had yet to talk to each other live about what was happening. The first few book clubs after my diagnosis, no one knew what to say, whether we should talk about it, but by this particular meeting, we knew that talking about it was fine. And they asked questions. What does cancer feel like? Am I scared? What is the worst part of the treatment? And I answered. They cared. They wanted more than the "oh, I am fine" answers. They wanted to really know, to understand this journey.

The biggest part of that evening for me was that they wanted me to remove my wig. Yes, I had posted pictures and I walked around my house without a wig, but, to purposely show friends what I looked like without my wig - I wasn't sure. But, the wig was itchy, and this was such a safe, secure, and loving environment that I thought - why not? So, I did. I removed my wig and sat with them for the evening...bald. And it was fine. A few held back tears; seeing me bald made the cancer so real. Importantly, they made me feel comfortable. Sitting without my wig with good friends was something I was no longer afraid to do.

Even as I write this, two and half years post treatment, I have to smile. We had book club last week. The first comment is always, "Oh my gosh, look at all your hair!"

CELEBRATING THE END OF CHEMO WITH FRIENDS

My sister Jennifer, who lives in Portland, OR wanted to take what we labeled the "Mack Truck" shift (when I would be most sick post chemo) in December, my last chemo, two weeks before Christmas. Jennifer has two young daughters, who were six and seven at the time. I didn't want Jennifer to come as I felt that she should be with her children during the holidays.

My mother explained that I should let Jennifer come because she so wanted to help me. It was so wonderful to have her here. Yet, I don't know that there was any way that we could have warned her of the situation.

I was really sick after the last chemo, barely able to lift my head. Sleeping for hours at a time. Waking up just long enough to apologize to Jennifer and tell her I wish I could take her out to dinner or shopping or something fun, but that I just couldn't.

Every time I woke up, Jennifer was baking cookies. The house smelled good, but nothing sounded good to me. Later she told me that she bakes when she is nervous or concerned and was she ever concerned!

Poor Jen! This was the first time she was seeing me since the cancer diagnosis. She knew I had been in the hospital after the last chemo. And now, she had taken on the mantle of helping me during this final, and what turned out to be very rough, treatment. In fact, it came out later that Jennifer was calling our mother and other sister multiple times a day, telling them what I was doing and asking what else she should do.

Donna

Back to the Infusion Room, where I started my last chemo. First of all, my blood was awesome! The counts hadn't been this good since my first chemo treatment. As a result, I am hoping that my reaction will be more like my first treatment as well. Time will tell, of course.

Patty came to bring me lunch and then take me home after this last chemo. She showed up with Christmas cookies for everyone at Infusion that day, although what I loved was the bottle of champagne she brought so that we could celebrate that last treatment. Now, why oh why did they not let us pop the cork there?

It is frigidly cold here today, and a pipe had burst not six feet from where I was sitting! The Infusion room started taking on a heck of a lot of water. Truth be told, I didn't hear it, but Patty did! She was right there. So, the Infusion staff jumped into action, taking all the blankets and towels they could find to sop up the water. Maintenance got there maybe 20 minutes later.

So, while I was feeling sorry for those in the building, I started feeling sorry for us in Infusion as well. You see, when you receive IV liquid for seven hours straight, frequent trips to the bathroom become necessities!

As I moved from my new chair to yet another new chair even farther away, I thought I would stop at the restroom. However, our clueless wonder here (Moi!) did not know that they had already turned off the water - and that they had turned it off for the entire building, meaning I couldn't flush the toilet. Trying to be gracious and ladylike about all of this, I quietly said to Patty that with the water off, the bathrooms weren't working, and we should make sure the nurses knew this for all the patients.

So, Patty being Patty, with her powerful voice called for a nurse to explain that the water was turned off in the bathrooms, and they were not working. How do you know, was the question. Because Donna can't flush the toilet, she announced to the entire room! Oh well - someone had to be the guinea pig!

91

Mom described a call when Jen said, "She had one sip of water and then she fell asleep again. What should I do?" Mom just encouraged her to bring me fresh water when I woke up again.

The thing about The Girls is that they were not only there for me, but they were there for each other. Not only did Jen have family to call, but the friends who stopped by offered to pick up things for her, run errands, or give her a chance to leave the house a little bit. Women supported women. In fact, it was good that Jennifer was baking as friends showed up left and right as I went through this last chemo. She was always able to greet them with homemade Christmas cookies!

To celebrate the end of chemo, Patty and Deborah came to visit. When the three of us are together, much laughter always ensues. Wine is also consumed at these get-togethers. This time, they brought champagne, for our celebration. We hung out in the sunroom, me lying on the couch, Jennifer serving cookies, Deborah and Patty telling stories that had us all laughing. I had one sip of champagne. It didn't really taste good, and I was too tired to sit up and drink it anyhow.

> **Donna**
>
> *Still swimming, but with a tad bit more energy today. Jennifer leaves tomorrow ☹. It has been great having her!! She just did everything.... another true angel in my life! Speaking of angels, Mom and Dad are coming to town tomorrow and will stay through Christmas.*
>
> *They weren't going to come till later in the week; however, things changed. You see, I'm still wiped out, exhausted, short of breath, nauseated, etc., etc. from this last chemo. Mom and Dad explained that I really get no vote regarding their visit. So, it was agreed to unanimously by everyone else that they should come. By everyone, I do mean everyone: the family and many friends who stopped by today...Kathy, Patty, Jackie, Steph, Jenni, Deborah, and a few others this chemo brain is forgetting.*
>
> *For the record, I thought I would be fine. ☺ But, you already knew that!*
>
> *Love to all, especially those angels looking out for me!*

Afterwards, Jennifer was dumbfounded. "These women stayed a few hours – and you stayed awake for much of it," she exclaimed. "You feel miserable but were laughing the entire time. You slept while they just kept right on talking and carrying on. " And Patty and Deborah - they brought Jennifer into the fold. Yes, cancer is serious, and I was quite sick. This was an enormous burden on my "baby" sister, but these friends and others were there to help her, as well as me, through it.

It Is Hard For Others

A friend who had undergone breast cancer explained to me that it would be much easier for me to go through the cancer than for my family and friends to watch me deal with it. They want to do something: what they want most is to take this burden from you, make you better. Yet, they can't.

This statement proved so true for my mother, as it was devastating for her to watch me undergo this illness and treatment. But, it was an important thing for me to know as well, to understand that others would need help in dealing with this.

Knowing how rough my cancer was on others, I decided that I would do what I could to make it easier. I would bring it up, I would laugh about things, I would point out the obvious. That way, if they wanted to ask questions, to talk about it, the door was open to them. If they didn't, that was fine as well.

It was Mary Beth who asked at one of our first book club get-togethers post diagnosis, can we talk about the elephant in the room? I realized that not everyone was willing to ask that question, so I let them know that my cancer was okay to discuss if they wanted to do so.

Not everyone wants to hear, wants to talk about it. That doesn't mean they don't want to help or be there. It simply means verbalizing it is not how they want to address it. If they didn't want to talk about it, we didn't. That was fine. I loved hearing about families and jobs and things other than cancer. That reminded me that there was a big world out there that did not revolve around my situation.

There is no one perfect answer about what to say or what to do when a friend or family member has cancer. Everyone is different and every journey is different. I now know people who never told a soul they had cancer. I, of course, did talk about it. My best advice on this topic? Be real. Be yourself. Let your friendship and love shine through.

ANGELS AMONG US

How do you really thank angels? My life was full of them as I went through this cancer journey. A simple thank you didn't seem to be enough. I couldn't figure out how to let them know how much I appreciated everything and how much they meant to me. And, yes, I did really think of them as angels as they would float in and handle something with great love and kindness.

Because it was the holiday season when my chemo was coming to an end, I decided to have an "Angel" party. Dear friends had decorated the house. The rest of the family was coming in town. My energy was coming back. And I could have everyone together to thank them a few days after Christmas.

Of course they all laughed at me. I was but three weeks post my last chemo. "You can't have a party," I heard, but, I ordered trays of food and hired servers. I couldn't do the work, but I could enjoy the company. I found lovely little angels, simple and elegant, and bought one for each friend. Jennifer wrapped all 30 of them while I was sleeping post chemo.

At the party, I handed them out, and I shared a story about each "angel" in my life, how he or she had helped, why each was special to me. When I finished, my nephew (who is studying music and piano in college) played Christmas carols, especially those featuring angels.

I loved that party. I loved it because I could visit with each person, share why each was so important to me, and connect all those who are special in my life. And, I was doing it as I was beginning to feel better. I was taking back a bit of control over my life with that little get-together.

I don't know that I will ever adequately thank my friends who were there for me, but, I always hope that as they look at their angels, they remember that they were, indeed, an angel to me, when I needed them most.

MEDICAL MYSTERIES

THE UNEXPECTED HOSPITAL TRIP

Truth be told, you might end up unexpectedly in the hospital while you go through cancer treatments. I showed up there a few different times and for one trip had to stay several nights.

You would think that I would have learned to pack an emergency bag – in case I did have to go to the hospital. However, I was in denial: I wasn't that sick, was I?

You know you will get tired from chemo, that your body will get physically fatigued. Constantly battling side

> **Judy**
>
> *A former cancer patient told me that there would be one chemo treatment that would make you feel as if you couldn't do this for one more day. For me that was chemo number 3. I laid in my bathtub and couldn't get warm, no matter what I did. My body ached and I did ask myself, why am I doing this? At that moment I thought about the simple thing she said to me to get through this. To remind yourself that many women before you have done this and you can, too.*

effects, your body doesn't have a chance to catch its breath and recover. So, it starts to shut down, find its own way to get the rest it deserves.

Unfortunately, chemo fatigue often results in a trip to the ER, to prop your body up and help it continue to work through the side effects. I learned the hard way that there are many things that you should have ready in case a trip to the hospital is required. If you have to go due to chemo fatigue, you may not be thinking, processing as clearly as normally. So, taking a few minutes in advance to pull everything together should the worse occur is advisable.

My first trip to the hospital, when the ambulance was called for me, my body was not physically working. In my head, I knew things like the hospital we had to go to, what my blood counts had been a few days ago, and the type of chemo I was on. But, for the life of me, I could not say the words or get the message to the EMTs. I learned the hard way the importance of having a little card or putting in writing the critical medical information, including:

- Name and address
- Doctor's name and preferred hospital
- Relative's name and phone number
- Current insurance
- The type of chemo currently on and the last chemo date
- The medicines currently on
- Most recent blood count numbers including WBC, RBC and platelet count (See the section below on Learning the Numbers for more information on blood counts.)

Once I was at the hospital for a bit and started to perk up, I realized that there were a number of other items that I should have brought with me. Personal items to consider for your bag include:

- A pill box with a few of each of your current medications. Anything you take that you have not brought with you will require a doctor's order. Of course, you will want to verify with the doctor that you can keep taking them, but it does simplify things if you have some with you.
- A wig, scarf, hat, or anything else that you typically wear on your head
- Some basic make-up, like lipstick or mascara
- A change or two of comfortable clothes, including underwear
- Lip balm and hand cream. Your skin will still be very dry.
- Cell phone, ipad, etc., and their chargers

- A list of contacts and their phone numbers (If your cell phone dies and you try to use the hospital phones, you will need the phone numbers. I speak from experience.)

A number of complications may cause a trip to the hospital. Chemo fatigue is a general description. Usually there are underlying causes for chemo fatigue, such as lack of nutrition or blood count changes that cause the significant fatigue.

LEARNING THE NUMBERS

One challenge of having cancer is having to learn what may be a new language....a medical language.

> *Donna*
>
> *Good Morning All....*
>
> *So, I must admit, I am surprised by how well I have handled this chemo so far. Days 3 and 4 have not proven to be too troublesome.*
>
> *Headaches have been the worst of the symptoms, and heck, I can get a headache just thinking about work. :) So, that is no big deal. They gave me a Neulasta shot 24 hours after chemo. Neulasta stimulates white blood cell growth, since the chemo works against white blood cell growth. A common side effect of the Neulasta is sore bones as the bones need to start working harder to produce the white blood cells. Yes, I did experience that effect as well. The big deal on this one is that I learned that each shot costs about $4000. WOW!*

All of a sudden, things that you have heard of but perhaps never thought about, like white blood cells and platelets, determine whether or not you will even get your next round of chemo. Even before your course of treatment starts, your care team will begin to treat the expected chemo side effects with various drugs. But the drugs can have side effects, too, so you are battling side effect after side effect.

People diagnosed with cancer have different approaches on how to handle the vast amount of medical information available regarding their illness. Some people want to know everything going on with their body, every last number and why it matters. Others feel that it is the doctor's role to worry about the numbers, that the patient's role is to do what he or she is told, not worry, rest, and get better.

I ended up somewhere in the middle, as many patients do. In the beginning I held back on studying the numbers, the drugs, etc. My doctors actually advised me to steer clear of the

---

Donna

I wish I could have honored my Mother's request and had a good, successful day at chemo. Unfortunately, that was not the case today. In fact, I could not even receive chemo today. The long story is this... I have been experiencing lots of bleeding, from my poor thumb to nosebleeds to the slightest little nick. So, of course I shared that with the doctor today, who was concerned as that is not normal.

They always check your blood work before doing chemo just in case, and today they took even more blood for a few extra tests. As it turns out my platelets are way too low. Apparently, most people have platelet counts of around 150,000 to 400,000. Chemo can be done at 100,000, but under that they get concerned. Mine were around 40,000, so, very, very low. Enough to really concern the doctors.

Without the platelets my blood won't clot. That explains all the bleeding - and why they were so concerned! Our game plan is to wait a week and try chemo next Monday instead.

Donna

Good evening all,

I was so tired last night that I forgot to share the most important piece of news I received on Friday regarding the mammogram. While the overall size of the tumor has not changed much, the density is greatly diminished. The oncologist is very pleased with that result! Because this means the chemo is working, we will stay on this treatment protocol. Of course, we can only do that if we figure out the blood issue.

I have just been so tired that I can hardly move it seems. Apparently, the low blood counts are driving this exhaustion. So, hopefully if we get the counts back in line, I will be in better shape and not get so tired.

Pushing back chemo this week most likely will change my entire chemo schedule, pushing everything back a week or so, perhaps more, depending on what we learn next week. That is what I get for trying to plan everything out so precisely! :-)

Of course, the good news is I should feel really good this weekend! No Mack Truck to contend with on Friday - YEAH!

---

internet; there is so much false and scary information out there. Furthermore, every body is different, so for all your studying, your findings may not even apply to you.

About half way through my chemo treatment, however, something went wrong with my blood, and I was not able to receive my next course as scheduled. When that happened, my entire approach to wanting to understand my numbers changed. This was a significant turning point because all of a sudden family and friends wanted to know what had happened to change the treatment. Quite frankly, I wanted to understand as well. What did the doctors see and know that caused them to change the schedule? As I learned more and more, I was able to help family and friends understand the situation as well.

As I learned the numbers, I learned that the blood really does tell the oncologists what is going on with your body at any given stage of treatment. Before my first chemo treatment, they drew quite a bit of blood, shared the results of the tests with me, and told me to save them. Little did I know how important that was! Throughout your treatment, your doctor will run regular blood counts to monitor your condition. As irregularities later started to show up in my blood, I could compare and ask questions, finding out where the problems were.

The first series of numbers I learned to really care about were the red blood cell count (RBC), white blood cell count (WBC), and platelet count.

> **Donna**
>
> *Arghhhhhh!!!!!*
>
> *Let's start with chemo. We couldn't do chemo today as my blood counts were even worse than last time. The platelets were 33,000 the first time they took the blood today and so they took it again. The counts were 32,000 when they took it the second time.*
>
> *They were hopeful that the test machine had erred, but no luck. Apparently, after chemo, blood takes a hit and then rebuilds itself. They are hoping that I am just slow to have my blood recover. They are finding that I am very sensitive to meds and that appears true for my blood as well. The game plan is for me to get chemo on Tues now. First they will take more blood, and we will hope that my platelet counts are up and we can do the chemo.*

As is typical, the chemo definitely damaged all three of these for me, resulting in a variety of side effects.

As their primary function, white blood cells destroy bacteria and viruses in the body. In other words, they keep us healthy. Chemo can slow down or even stop the body's ability to create white blood cells, compromising the patient's ability to fight off infection. This is why chemo patients are advised to stay clear of those who are ill with even a cold or the flu. If you do get a cold, flu, or other infection, your WBCs work to get rid of the infection, but with limited WBCs because of treatment, it will take you longer to get over such an illness than it would a well person. Additionally, because the WBCs are going after the infection, that puts further demands on your body, and may cause your counts to drop even more. Before you know it, your next chemo treatment may be delayed, something you definitely don't want. The reverse can happen as well: A body may react to a toxic medicine or chemo by creating a significant number of WBCs. Too much production of WBCs is an indication that something else is amiss in your body. Either way, watching the WBCs helps you and your doctor understand how your body is processing the treatments.

> **Donna**
>
> *Happy Monday Everyone....*
>
> *In the good news department, I am sitting at chemo, getting chemo! Yeah! By going off the acid reflux medicine, I went from a platelet count of 44,000 to a count this week of 175,000. The average range is from 150,000 to 400,000, so I am back in the normal range. Therefore, they could do the chemo.*

Red blood cells are another critical cell count that the doctors watch. These cells carry oxygen throughout the body and carbon dioxide back to the lungs to be exhaled. If your RBC count is down as a result of chemo, there are fewer cells carrying the carbon dioxide out and transporting the oxygen that is needed for all parts of your body to work. In fact, something as simple as a lower RBC count can account for some of the exhaustion you feel during and after your chemo.

Platelets are another very important part of the blood as they clump together to clot when needed. Without enough platelets, even something as simple as a bloody nose may take longer to stop.

Before each and every chemo treatment your blood will be taken so that the doctors can run a Complete Blood Count (CBC). This test measures the WBCs,

> **Donna**
>
> *Greetings from Chemo....*
>
> *Thought I would give everyone the update.*
>
> *Yes, I am getting chemo today, but just part of it. My counts are ever so slightly improved. The platelets are at 53,000 and the hemoglobin at 8.9. They are giving me Taxotere only today. The Carboplatin (chemo drug) is what causes the blood counts to go down, the severe exhaustion, etc., etc. So the plan is for me to just skip the Carboplatin this cycle, allowing my body to recover, and get the full chemo treatment on my last course of treatment.*
>
> *Meanwhile, we will not do the blood transfusion tomorrow. I am just above the cut off level for a transfusion. So, they are hoping that by not giving me the Carboplatin, my blood can repair itself. In other news, we got the MRI results back and it is good news. The tumor has shown a significant decrease in size. Yeah!!*

RBCs, and platelets, and the results are often provided before the chemo even begins. Another blood test that is performed before chemo is a chemistry screen. It measures the levels of different substances in your body, such as electrolytes. The chemistry screen can tell your doctor about your general health, look for certain problems, and help determine whether a particular treatment is working or not. One final important blood test usually done before treatment is a measurement of your cancer "marker." There is a variety of types of cancer markers, and they are dependent on the type of cancer you have. In a broad sense, a cancer marker is something - a chemical, a protein, etc. - that is associated with your type of cancer. Most people have these chemicals or proteins in them whether they have cancer or not, so looking at a cancer marker may not tell a doctor that you have cancer.

However, monitoring the trends of the marker may show such things as whether your treatments appear to be working or not. Therefore, watching the changes in cancer markers is an important consideration for your doctors.

Your medical oncologist is typically the one constantly monitoring your blood. However, that does not mean the other doctors on your team are not following it closely as well, such as your radiation oncologist monitoring how your body is handling the treatment he or she is providing. If surgery is part of your plan, your surgeon will check blood counts to ensure that your body is capable of handling the operation. In fact, right before surgery I always had additional blood drawn for this purpose.

To Ponder

One of the most critical things that your doctors will watch is your "numbers," your blood counts. Those numbers can provide a myriad of insights from potential diagnoses to reasons for side effects. How much you dig into the numbers yourself is naturally your choice. For some of you, knowing your numbers and watching along with the doctors may give you a sense of control. For others of you, letting someone else focus on the numbers is one less thing for you to worry about. Regardless of your approach, know that these numbers are vital in determining the course of your treatment.

Donna

Good Morning Everyone...

So, I promised a more detailed update on what really happened, so let's give that a whirl this morning. If we start with Thanksgiving, you may recall that all I did was sleep, sleep, sleep (dreaming of turkey, of course, Mom!). When I was up, I would get very short of breath just walking from one room to another. I was light-headed as we did some things, especially as I bent down to help with Christmas decorations. No putting the skirt around the tree for me this year!

Monday came and I had a bit of color. We thought I was improving. Mom and Dad went back home to Ohio. I had a very busy day at work, although I didn't go in. I was on the phone the entire time. As I got to the end of the day, I called the Infusion room as something just wasn't right. My brain wasn't processing, and I was short of breath as I said just a few words. I would walk from chair to chair and then sit and rest. I couldn't even get across the room. The Infusion Room Chemo Nurse was worried and asked if the ER might be an option. I thought I would be ok (of course!), but, she did schedule an appointment for the next day.

By about 7 that evening, I felt like I couldn't put two words together. That is when Jackie (my neighbor) called 911, and the hospital stint started. So, what do we think happened? Officially, they called it "chemo fatigue." There were a number of things occurring, though, anemia being one of them. So, my hemoglobin was low. That is the protein that carries the oxygen. The hemoglobin attaches to our red blood cells, and those were also low in me. So, net of that was that oxygen was having a hard time attaching and going through me. Someone asked if I should have been put on O2. I wasn't, because as I understand it, I was getting O2; I just wasn't getting it through me. But that wasn't all of it. I also had very low potassium, so they had to give me a bunch of that as well. The oncologist was surprised at how quickly I came back after they started IVs, transfusion, etc., which led her to wonder if I was also somewhat dehydrated. But I had five 16oz bottles of water on Monday, so that probably wasn't it. Most likely, because I hadn't been feeling well, I hadn't eaten much. (True.) Therefore, it wasn't dehydration per se but more a lack of electrolytes that also caused some problems.

The net of it is, we will never fully understand everything that happened on that Monday. My summary is that my body entered the Bermuda Triangle - low blood counts, low potassium, and low electrolytes and presto-change-o, I was a mess.

One of the lovely nurses (Lisa, I think) explained it in a good way. I was sleeping so much because my body was trying to recover from the chemo on its own. But, when it just couldn't recover on its own, systems went down as sort of a red alert that it needed help. Help arrived, and we are off and running again.

OTHER COMPLICATIONS

Another complication of treatment, though most unladylike to discuss, is diarrhea. Understand that your chemo, your medications, so many things impact your digestion. From the very beginning, when you swallow your first morsel of food, if you have dry mouth, you may not have the initial enzymes that start the digestion process. Of course, as the food then goes through your system, it may find other digestive parts and pieces that are not working properly. The results, well, they can be ugly. Also, they can be constant, and the cause of still other issues.

First of all, of course, you may not be getting the nutrition you need. The issues can get compounded. You don't want to eat because of what happens, the diarrhea. You don't want to eat because your mouth is sore, from dry mouth. You don't want to eat because everything tastes metallic. And, you just simply do not have an appetite. Because of this, you may not be getting in enough nutrition, or the right nutrition. That, of course, can impact your digestion. You couple poor nutrition with the medications and chemo, and it is easy to see why diarrhea can become a constant pain in the... well, you know.

Another big issue with diarrhea is the loss of electrolytes in your body. Electrolytes are essential minerals in your blood or other body fluids, such as potassium, sodium, calcium, and magnesium. Electrolytes regulate many body functions, like nerve and muscle function, body Ph, and blood pressure, to name a few. So, a loss of electrolytes can put your blood and body systems out of whack as well. Products like Gatorade, often used by athletes, can pump up the electrolytes. Another good option is Pedialyte, given to children when they are sick with flu. I tended to prefer Pedialyte, especially because it can be purchased as popsicles, which somehow just tasted a lot better to me. In the chapter Food, I address more fully how to get the nutrition you need.

And lest we forget. Another problem with diarrhea is that your "bum" may just become really sore. A friend who really suffered with this challenge swore by Boudreaux's Butt Paste. Initially developed to treat diaper rash in babies, it is very soothing should you find yourself sore with this complication.

A Hospital Visit

The problem with any of these complications is that they can potentially land you in the hospital. Understand, if you are admitted to the hospital, you are going in as a cancer patient. On one level you know that. For the doctors and caregivers at the hospital, this causes a level of concern that you may not have experienced before.

Donna

Let's call this post....Lessons Learned from the Hospital!

Lesson 1: You do not go to the hospital to sleep.
How do I know this? Because I am getting ready to stay for night number two and have slept, what, two to three hours? (Kristina might know!) See, at the hospital you are really, really busy with nurses and doctors and more nurses, and CAT scans and doppler ultrasounds, and all sorts of stuff. And that doesn't include all the visitors. It is impossible to sleep when you are catching up with everyone.

But, here is the real problem....my cats are at home, and I can't sleep without them. How does one possibly sleep amidst all of this?

Lesson #2: Always bring your wig and make-up on the ambulance.
Because, once you start feeling better, you are really going to be disappointed that you don't have them! Yes, ambulance. So last night I couldn't catch my breath, I was dizzy, light-headed, and most importantly (in my mind), couldn't put words together. Even stringing two words together wasn't working well. So, when my lovely neighbor, Jackie, checked in on me and saw what was going on, she called 911, no question asked! With what little focus I had, I directed us to take my wallet so I had my insurance card and to take us to St. John's Mercy where my cancer was being treated. Who knew that 24 hours later, with lots of IVs, pills, shots, and a blood transfusion to boot, that I would realize that the most important items - my make-up and my wig - we had left at home? (And we know what I look like without those two key items!!)

Lesson #3: Hospitals are paid to worry about every little thing.
Ohio fans, can we all say Histoplasmosis? How about Ohio Valley? You know what I am talking about - don't you? For those out of the loop....when you live in the southern part of Ohio there is a special fungus that grows that often shows up as a spot on a lung. Totally nothing – if, in fact, you are familiar with Histoplasmosis. I grew up in southern Ohio, so it is commonplace for me. But, fast forward to me, arriving at the hospital. My leg is quite swollen, and the doctors are concerned that, given the other symptoms, I might have a blood clot. So, they immediately take half of my remaining blood for tests, and they do a CAT scan of my chest. What do they find? A spot. Now, from their perspective, this is not good, and they are worried. A cancer patient with a spot on her lung. I would have said, "Oh heavens" if I could have strung those two words together last night. Finally today, I explained to no fewer than four doctors here our little Ohio deal. Since they are all Missouri doctors here, they are not as familiar. So, they are doing their due diligence, checking out my CAT scan from July (when I had the pneumonia) and comparing the spot they found then with the spot they now found. They want to be sure that nothing has changed. I am quite cool with that. They are worried; I am not. But, I am staying until tomorrow so that we can calm their worries. And, yes, that is the right thing to do.

Lesson #4: You have to have wings to work on an Oncology Hematology Floor.
And by that, I mean angel wings! The nurses and techs here are really something special!! Always with a smile, maybe a little goofiness, and tons of kindness. How does God create such special people? Kristina, Chelsey, Randy, Lisa...I am talking about you! They work with really sick people day in and day out and somehow find the energy to be lovely every moment of every day. Those are the big lessons for the day.

110

As you know, my belief is that living like a lady is very much about attitude. You can choose to lie around and feel sorry for yourself. Or, you can choose to smile and think about others. That is hard when you feel so lousy. Yet, it makes all the difference in the world.

While on the oncology floor, I met some amazing caregivers. Even though I couldn't put together more than a few words, I tried to get to know them. The more I spoke with them, the more I understood what a difficult job they have. The people who deal with cancer patients are often dealing with very, very sick people. When you are that sick, it is easy to take it out on those that care for you.

Even in the hospital, I chose to smile. No doubt, I was very sick, but, a little smile to those trying to care for me opened me up to some absolutely beautiful people, and I am the richer for it.

> *Donna*
>
> *A very brief update to say I am HOME! Yeah!!*
>
> *I will miss all my new angels – well, friends – well, angels - well...you get it :-) from the hospital. But I am glad to be back at the St. Louis Heckler ranch! More later.... but for now, thanks again for all the support....*
>
> *Donna*

A CORNUCOPIA OF MEDICATION

When you find out you have cancer, you know that medicine will be involved. What you may not understand is exactly how much! There were times that I would open up my hall closet, absolutely stunned by the array of medications in there. So, I had two or three things I was used to taking on a regular basis before cancer, but the amount of medications I had going through treatments was simply amazing to me.

Obviously, I can't tell you every single medication that you may take. You have a different cancer, your situation is different. My point in this chapter is not to tell you about every medication, but rather to share what you might expect as you face your various treatments. The sheer number and types of medications can be overwhelming. So, the following is a discussion of some of the more common medications that may be prescribed for you.

To get the journey started, be sure to tell your oncologist everything you are already taking, including supplements. I was able to continue on my everyday medications; however, I was told to stop all supplements and vitamins. Until they

> **Donna**
>
> *Good Evening All....*
>
> *What a day - first time with chemo and it was a long ordeal. We arrived this morning at 9 a.m. and didn't leave until 4:15 p.m. - can you imagine???*
>
> *It was three different chemo drugs and a few other drugs dripped in to handle the nausea. So, seven hours later I got to head for home. In some wonderful news, my sister Karen was able to return to St. Louis with me yesterday from Indiana. So, she spent the day with me at chemo. It was so great having her support!*
>
> *All things being equal, I feel pretty good, given everything that went on. I have a headache, but that is it. Stay tuned for days 3 and 4 as I hear those get a bit more difficult. But, time will tell...*
>
> *Hugs to all....*

knew what was really driving and impacting my cancer, they did not want anything else to cloud or impact my condition.

CHEMOTHERAPY

There are multiple kinds of chemotherapies, and they do different things. Of course, what is prescribed for you is dependent upon you cancer, your history, and what your doctor recommends for you. However, one thing that is common is that chemo can cause significant side effects. As a result, you may be placed on a variety of medications to handle the side effects.

> **Donna**
>
> *Arghhhhh....this headache!!! We have magical drugs for nausea. I think I need to invent something magical for headaches now.*
>
> *Enjoy this lovely weekend all....*

Nausea is one of the most challenging and common side effects of chemo. I was given some initial anti-nausea medication by infusion, before each of my chemo treatments. In addition, the nurses outlined the medications that I was to take on the days following my chemo treatments. Their schedule even had a reminder for when I was to go to the pharmacy to pick up the medications, because, as I learned later, sometimes people are just so wiped out from chemo that they forget to pick up these follow-up medications, which are so critical for nausea management.

It is important to follow the regimen very carefully for the medications to be effective in

> **Donna**
>
> *Fire-up - Chemo number two is now complete!!*
>
> *So, first things first: I feel fine. But, it was another long day. We were there again from 9 a.m. until around 4 p.m. But, through the course of the day, we got lots of tidbits of good news. :-)*
>
> *Most encouraging is that the tumor has already shrunk some! YEAH.*

eliminating the sense of nausea. I was provided three prescriptions used strictly to prevent the nausea: Emend Dose Pack, Decadron (a steroid), and Compazine (for use if the first two medications did not work). Fortunately, I found these medications to work exceptionally well for me, and I never had any issue with nausea.

However, I did learn that I had to identify the drugs in a manner that would make it easier for those helping me to know which ones were required and when. I grouped medications into separate plastic containers. One container held my post chemo medications for daytime. A second held my everyday medications that I could still take. A third held the nighttime post chemo medications. I also kept the schedule of drugs posted in the kitchen so that anyone stopping by or helping out could easily look to see what was required that day.

I received an injection of Neulasta the day following each chemo, used to stimulate white blood cell production, since chemo damages those cells. A significant side effect of the Neulasta can be deep bone aches. White

> **Donna**
> They are taking me off of all acid reflux medicine. One bad side affect of chemo is horrible acid reflux. In fact, on some days I could hardly stand sipping water. However, the medications they have me on for that may be depleting/ harming my platelets. So, we will stop all those medicines for a week and see if that helps to correct the platelet count. Now, the downside, of course, could be horrible reflux again, but I will just have to tolerate that if it solves the platelet situation.

blood cells are produced in the bone, which explains why a drug designed to increase cell production would also cause bone pain.

Another drug I was prescribed was Ativan, an anti-anxiety, for the evening. I explained that I was not anxious and did not need it, but the doctors and nurses argued heartily with me explaining that Ativan would help me to sleep, assistance many patients need post chemo. It would also help with nausea, so I was advised to take one at night in the days following chemo treatments. The doctors also explained that many people do become anxious, even depressed, upon having chemo, and Ativan is one of the medications commonly prescribed. Another common side effect with chemo is headaches. In my case, an anti-nausea medication was causing the headaches. A change in medication quickly solved that issue for future chemo treatments.

I did learn to keep close track of the side effects I experienced and bring the list to the oncologist on my next visit. In response, she would adjust dosages or even change medications to eliminate the effects I was having.

Acid reflux is another common

> **Donna**
>
> *I have a new little side effect to report. I shake now, my hands especially. So what do I do? With my "chemo brain" today, I chose soup for lunch. I got through about half the bowl of soup, with a quarter going in me and a quarter going on me!*
>
> *So, this shaking is a bit concerning. However, my speculation is that it is because I am not eating enough. Like virtually nothing. Remember I mentioned the acid reflux? Now that I am off the medicine, I have more energy, but everything I consume, including water, hurts. So, this is easy to fix - don't eat or drink right? But, then I get the shakes. Oh chemo nurses, what do you recommend now?*

side effect from chemo as well. Most likely, you will go home with a recommendation of what to take for that on the detailed schedule your nurses provide. As I had struggled with acid reflux even before treatment, the oncology team worked to find the best over-the-counter option for me. Unfortunately, it impacted my blood counts, so I was taken off that particular drug.

Another common side effect is general body aches. Typically, the infusion room nurses will work with you to use ibuprofen (Advil/Motrin) to relieve body aches and acetaminophen (Tylenol) to relieve the headaches, coordinating a schedule to minimize the side effects associated with them, while maximizing their ability to manage the body aches and pains. Commonly, you will be advised NOT to take aspirin as it can interfere with your blood, which is already being damaged by the treatments. Of course, your doctor will make recommendations on the medications that will be best for you.

Learning about all the medicines while I was receiving my first chemo was overwhelming. I

> **Donna**
>
> *Good evening everyone,*
>
> *Well, things are a bit interesting here. Turns out I have caught a little cold. Usually not a big thing for me, but when on chemo, it is an entirely different story!! I called the doctors to let them know, and they were concerned. Concerned enough to put me on antibiotics for 14 days!! Can you believe it??? Truth be told, I don't feel great. But a cold on top of the fatigue from chemo makes for a really tired me. :-)*

was nervous about not managing them correctly, and I feared headaches and nausea would be the result. During that first chemo, the nurses sat with me and wrote out a schedule, indicating days and times that I was to take the different medications. They advised that I keep that schedule as we would do the exact same things after each chemo treatment. It was hard to process everything - getting my first chemo, being in an infusion room the first time, understanding the medications required and their timing.

While I did not find the cancer, itself, to be painful, depending on the cancer, many people do. Your oncologist can keep not only the side effects from the chemo at bay, but also the pain from the cancer if you are struggling with that. However, make sure you speak up at your appointments, sharing even the littlest thing so that the pain and side effects can be managed.

The rule of thumb for chemo, I was told, is that your first call should always be to the oncology doctors and nurses for virtually everything. If I had to travel for work, ask the nurse first. When I thought I had picked up a little cold, the oncology team was the first to know. Your blood is taking a beating during chemo, so the slightest little thing can cause an infection or a cold you could typically otherwise ward off. Of course, the antibiotics or other meds your oncology team uses to treat these infections can have their own side effects that will need to be managed. A big one with antibiotics can be constipation or diarrhea. So, if your chemo is already triggering that in you, recognize that additional antibiotics may serve to exacerbate the condition.

Another consideration you might face is how treatment will affect health issues you already have. Before my cancer diagnosis I had had several surgeries to repair a badly broken leg and was still doing rehab on it. Once my cancer treatments started, I noticed right away that my leg was the most susceptible to the pain, discomfort, and exhaustion from treatment. I explained to my orthopedic surgeon that I felt my leg was a "leading indicator," using a business metaphor, that when anything was done through a treatment, my leg was the first to feel it. He explained that he preferred the metaphor of the "canary in the coal mine." Regardless of the phrase, the piece to watch out for is that if you have other physical ailments, they may trouble you even more on chemo. My doctor sometimes had to treat the pain in my ankle or knee exacerbated by chemo and other medication I was taking. Ice worked on occasion, but I took additional pain medications when it didn't suffice.

SURGERY

Should you have to go through surgery, you may be prescribed a variety of other medications. Of course, the big issue post surgery is managing the pain, especially if the surgeon has cut through muscle or inner organs. Drugs such as Vicodin and Percocet are commonly prescribed as is a combination of painkiller and ibuprofen. Keeping a list of medications and when you take each of them is critical, especially post surgery, as pain medications can make you very groggy.

> **Donna**
>
> *Good morning gang!*
>
> *No big pondering thoughts today as I can't seem to get my mind past the pain. It is hard to believe that I came home just a week ago yesterday after surgery two days in a row, a double mastectomy and initial reconstruction. On days like today I say, yep, I feel it.*
>
> *I got off the Vicodin and switched to extra strength Tylenol around Monday of this week. I am trying to stay with the Tylenol as much as possible (cause then I can have a little sip of wine at night - and with Mom pouring, trust me, it is an itty, bitty, sip. :-)).*
>
> *I think I feel it so much more today because we did a lot again yesterday. I took a shower - that's a big event in my life these days. I put on make-up, even all my eye make-up. (I count that as a good bit of therapy as I have to hold my arms up to do that, of course.). I also was back at the plastic surgeon, and she is very pleased. It is coming along well, and the swelling is going down. Anyhow, with all that activity yesterday, no wonder things are a bit "ouchy" today. :-)*
>
> *So, the pain is really worse on the left side. Of course, that is where the cancer was, so that is to be expected. Remember when you were a kid and you fell and skinned your knee? Then a day or two later you were running again, and it felt like it opened up a bit. That's what this reminds me of. But, unless we tie my arms down, I don't see the pain stopping any time soon.*

In the days immediately following surgery, you may sleep a lot. Driving may be on hold for some time depending upon medication, soreness, and range of motion issues. As you proceed to several days to a week past surgery, you may still find yourself groggy from the pain medications. As you start to feel better, you may want to begin driving again. Of course, your muscles will have to heal to a point where they can handle the quick reactions needed for driving, so make sure you connect with your doctor first on that. I quickly learned that my work would also be quite limited while I was on the pain medications. I had neither the focus nor the energy to respond to questions or discussions in meetings, even though I was feeling better.

> **Donna**
> *So, the negotiation has started (prompted by me), and the doctors said I may be able to begin working from home in a little bit, after 10-14 days or so. I guess pain medicine may be one of the big limiting factors.*
>
> *Please, how much pain medicine will I need?*

A special call-out to women going through a mastectomy or double mastectomy with reconstructive surgery. Often, during the mastectomy or double mastectomy, the plastic surgeon will insert what are called expanders, devices that expand or stretch the skin/muscle so that it is ready to accept the implants you receive later. Fills, when the expanders are filled with fluid to expand them, are then done every few weeks and can be rather painful as the muscles are stretched. However, typically a drug such as Valium is prescribed to manage the muscle spasms or pain that may result. Much more on the process of expansion is discussed in the chapter Surgical Insights for Those with Breast Cancer.

A word of caution about your pain medications at home: They are prime targets for stealing. Unfortunately, I found this out the hard way as I had people coming and going, from those checking on me to a clerk delivering groceries. Keep your pain medications in a safe, concealed place. In the end, you don't want to be in pain only to discover that the medications have been taken by someone else.

RADIATION

Radiation is a bit of a different animal in that there typically is no pain during the actual treatment. Significant side effects, though, include burn and damage to the area receiving the treatment. Medications are typically about managing side effects.

Infection is the main concern when there is a burn. Your doctors will keep a close eye out for infection, and at the first sign, begin to treat it with antibiotics. I was on quite a few different antibiotics through the course of my treatments, combatting colds, flu, and other infections. Other women I interviewed had the same experience: antibiotics often prescribed to treat infections.

Keeping infections at bay is critical as you undergo radiation as they further tax your body. Recognizing

> **Donna**
> Feeling great, doing too much, having fun, but oh this pesky infection. It is now covering the entire left side of my chest. They had me on two antibiotics since last week, but it got worse over the weekend. So, I was back at the doctor today, and she put me on Cipro. Let's hope it works its magic on me!

and bringing potential infection symptoms to your doctor early is important. Your body will be quite fatigued from the radiation, itself. You don't want your treatments limited or postponed because of added fatigue, so addressing infections immediately is crucial. Fatigue is discussed in detail in the chapter I Am Sooo Tired.... Energy and Fatigue.

Another significant side effect of radiation is scar tissue. A friend of mine going through radiation for throat cancer had to be hospitalized with a feeding tube, in order to complete her treatments, due to the burn and scar tissue. For those eventually undergoing breast

Donna

Hello Everyone...

A bit of a more technical medical update today.

Radiation is going well, and I am feeling better this week than I have in a number of weeks. We figured out the rash - or I should say, I figured out the rash. It, in fact, is NOT the radiation already. It also is not the detergent for the hospital gowns. It appears I had an allergic reaction to a medication. They put me on a drug as I started radiation as that has been found to minimize inflammation and reduce scar tissue development with expanders.

I had mentioned the rash to the radiation team, but since the drug is an anti-inflammatory, they didn't think it was the culprit. But, by last evening, my face was fiery red, along with my chest and arms. I looked up the drug, and sure enough, a rash is an allergic reaction that people can have to it. By then, it was about 9 p.m., so I called the pharmacist and asked him what he thought. He said skip it tonight and see what happens. By the time I woke up the next morning, the rash had started to clear from my face. I spoke with the radiation nurses, and they are keeping me off it.

reconstruction, your medical team may try to limit scar tissue through the use of medication, as that can impact the reconstruction results you can achieve. I was put on a drug that had proven effective at limiting scar tissue for some women; however, I had a serious allergic response to it and so couldn't continue using it.

Radiation can cause significant scar tissue to develop at the point of treatment. Your oncology team will work to manage that side effect in order to limit its impact on your other treatments or life in the future.

Post-Treatment

You finish treatment and think thank heavens, all is done. But, not quite. Often patients have to take medications for several years following treatment. Of course, it goes without saying that you should take them. However, as you approach Year 3 or 4 post treatment, and you feel like your "old" self (with the exception of the side effects of a particular drug), you may be tempted to stop taking the medication. Don't do it! There is a medical rationale for the use of the drugs post treatments and not taking them is tempting fate. Take the medications!

We typically hear about this with women recovering from breast cancer who take Tamoxifen for a minimum of five years and up to ten. Side effects, which can include significant hot flashes and intestinal distress, can get old. Depending on the type of cancer, a woman may also be put on an aromatase inhibitor that can limit the production of estrogen for post-menopausal women. Should you be on a drug post cancer treatment and find yourself with unpleasant side effects, be sure to discuss these with your doctor. Often times there are other medications that can be tried. Alternatively, supplement and diet choices may minimize the side effects. One great trick I discovered for hot flashes is Hot Girl Pearls. These oversized fake pearls are filled with a gel and come in a pouch. You keep them in the freezer until needed for a quick cool down. Out and about for the day, take the frozen pouch with you, and it will keep the pearls cold for a few hours, should those hot flashes hit again. Of course, ask your oncologist about other medical options for handling the side effects and living like the lady you are, now that the hard part of your treatments is completed.

MEDICATION DISPOSAL

You may need more than just a medicine cabinet to store the cornucopia of medications you will be prescribed during your cancer journey. However, once you have completed your various treatments, disposing of your medications properly is also critical. You do not want the medications falling into the wrong hands and potentially harming someone else, nor do you want them poisoning the environment.

More and more pharmacies have medicine take-back programs. Many community government, fire, or police stations offer this service to residents as well.

I enlisted the services of a dear friend, a nurse, who culled through all of my medication and took those I no longer needed to a local pharmacy, which was happy to take them so that they did not end up in the wrong hands.

As you live like a lady through your cancer, you will find yourself on a number of prescriptions for everything from managing illness and side effects to preventing potential side effects. These drugs - an essential part of your treatment - should be taken as directed, and then disposed of properly so that they help you while not harming others.

SURGICAL INSIGHTS FOR THOSE WITH BREAST CANCER

Surgery is always a traumatic experience for an individual, from the emotional fear and concern regarding outcomes and possible risks of the surgery, itself, to the physical pain. Breast cancer surgery comes with its own particular concerns and considerations.

DECISION POINTS

It took me a long time before I understood that there are two typical ways of thinking about breast cancer surgery: save as much of the breast as possible or remove fear of future problems by removing the entire breast. Decisions around breast cancer surgery have their start in your own fundamental philosophy.

To explain these philosophical differences, I can share the story of my friend Kathy, who went to my surgical appointments with me. In her mind, there was no doubt that everything must be done to conserve or save the breast, mine in this case, or any woman's. She was pushing the surgeon on the possibility of a lumpectomy for me so that my breast could be conserved as much as possible.

The challenge was, I just didn't care about that. I didn't care about saving my breast; I wanted both of them gone because I did not want to worry about breast cancer again. Kathy could not understand my mindset. It was in the exploration of these fundamental differences that I began to learn that there really are two different philosophies.

The doctors have since told me that these absolute mindsets are very common – everyone seems to fall into one or the other camp.

I start with this, because you need to think about what camp you fall into. Neither is, on its face, right or wrong: the question is, which philosophy is right for you? If you want to save your breast as much as possible, tell your doctors that. They can then help construct a course of action that is medically sound but will also meet your conservation need. If saving your breast is not a primary issue for you, tell your doctor that as well. Because saving the breast was not my concern, a double mastectomy was a surgical procedure that my doctor and I could explore.

Kathy and I had to agree to disagree. She could never wrap her head around me choosing to have a double mastectomy. I could never wrap my head around trying to save my breast, when it would mean carrying around the fear of recurrence. At our very core, we did not have the same beliefs. And that is completely ok. I just had to understand my core belief in order to proceed correctly for me.

Understanding your core belief then allows you to make further surgical decisions. Your oncology surgeon will guide

> **Donna**
>
> *I want to share my good news. Prayer works. And thank you to everyone for your loving support and prayers.*
>
> *You see, yesterday as I met with the surgeon, she could no longer feel the tumor! In fact, while we knew the MRI showed very positive results, she shared even more. The MRI picked up shadows, which could be scar tissue or cysts or even little tumor cells, but nothing like the 10cm worth of tumor they found earlier.*
>
> *The chemo worked! It did a number on me, but it worked. One more treatment on Monday. And, yes, we are still doing that chemo. Protocol calls for six treatments and we will do six.*
>
> *So, where do we go from here? There is still surgery to go through. But the idea of a lumpectomy is now a possibility. We didn't really see that as an option before. I may still end up going the mastectomy route. But, **that becomes a decision, not a necessity.***
>
> *With much love,*
>
> *Donna*

you initially in what options you have for removal of the cancer. Type, location, severity of your cancer will all factor into treatment decisions.

One thing to understand is that there is virtually no difference in survivor rates or recurrence between a mastectomy and a lumpectomy when followed with radiation.

Quickly upon meeting with the oncology surgeon, you will want to meet with your reconstructive surgeon. Often a plastic surgeon, he or she will advise you on what can be done to help you look "normal" after your cancer removal. These two pieces (cancer removal and breast reconstruction) need to be considered together, as overwhelming as that may seem. Unfortunately, your treatments may limit what can be done from a reconstruction perspective, so it is critical to get that information up front.

TYPES OF CANCER REMOVING SURGERIES

Doctors choose from among several core types of surgeries to remove your cancer. The simplest and least invasive is the lumpectomy. As its name implies, it removes the "lump" or the cancer, but does not remove the entire breast. Typically a lumpectomy is done in conjunction with radiation and for those with smaller tumors.

Women with larger tumors sometimes have neoadjuvant therapy, which in simplest terms is doing chemo prior to surgery in an effort to reduce the size of the tumor. If the size goes down due to the therapy, the option may exist to have a lumpectomy. Depending on the type of cancer, you may still have some lymph nodes removed with a lumpectomy. The procedure can be done in some cases as an outpatient procedure.

The second core type of surgery is the mastectomy, which is removal of the entire breast. When both breasts are removed, whether there is cancer in the second breast or not, it is considered a double mastectomy. The mastectomy (single or double) is major surgery and typically done under general anesthetic with an overnight hospital stay required. Commonly lymph nodes are removed with the mastectomy in an effort to determine if the cancer has begun to move into the lymphatic system.

So, why choose one over the other? It goes back to your philosophy to a large extent. If you want to conserve your breast as much as possible, there is an option for you. If conserving your breast is not as significant a factor, there are options for you as well.

Donna

A little update tonight on the cancer treatment. I went to the surgeon today so we could start thinking about a surgery date and get our "plan" in place. However, I am quickly learning that planning doesn't really work with cancer.

I have a slight change to my chemo schedule and will have chemo on Friday. The hope is that my bad "Mack" truck type of day will be before Thanksgiving in that way. The surgeon wants another MRI, so we will do that Friday morning before chemo.

Because there are two main tumors, she wants to see if the smaller one is gone. If so, we may be able to do the lumpectomy. The type of surgery will influence when I have it as well.

The surgeon will also speak to the radiation oncologist so we can see whether radiation will be needed. Typically with a lumpectomy there is radiation, but with a mastectomy, radiation is not always required. The surgeon is concerned that because my cancer was stage 3 and because of the size, I may need radiation regardless.

Finally, they are setting me up with a plastic surgeon. Often they do the first part of the reconstruction at the same time that they do the mastectomy. But there are all sorts of limitations: radiation must be completed before reconstruction, I must be off chemo a certain number of weeks before reconstruction, etc., etc.

The net of all this is, if you think God laughs when we plan, you should have heard the doctors! :-) The doctors all need to talk, and then they will decide what course to take. I trust them, and they are outstanding. It is just this little "control" issue I have that is troublesome.

Hopefully we will have more news on the treatment approach come Friday. But, I better not hold my breath. :-)

Love to all,

Donna

In the end, my cancer had been nearly 10 cm in size, larger than a tennis ball, so a lumpectomy, though possible, was probably not the best course of action for me. Because I was not fighting to conserve my breast as much as possible, the double mastectomy was a good option for me.

Margins

When I first started to talk to surgical oncologists, I kept hearing about "margins." In fact, the surgeon I ended up going to was recommended because she gets really good "margins." But, what are margins and why do we care?

Donna

Let's entitle this entry "Come Heck or High Water". We finished chemo! Dog gone it – we did it. It is done. For that we celebrate. But, the day left some questions as well.

Dear friend Deborah was here bright and early to take me to chemo, where my oncologist started by saying she didn't understand why the surgeon said she couldn't feel the tumor anymore because she (the oncologist) could. She said it was smaller for sure, but not that much smaller. The net of it is, we will know more when they take it out – the true size left, etc., etc.

I share this because it is part of the journey. The highs, the lows, but mostly the unknowns. I keep thinking of what one of my first bosses said back many a year ago. After I agreed with him on something, he said that if we all agree, then some of us aren't needed. By the way, he concluded, he wasn't going anywhere. ☺ It is true. Marketing doesn't always agree with Finance, who doesn't always agree with HR, but among all of us, we can help a company succeed. I guess the surgeon may not agree with the oncologist, who may not agree with the radiologist, but among all of them, we will get to the right answer and get me well. I will just go with that philosophy until I hear differently.

Margins are basically the area around the tumor. The surgeons, based on skill, experience, and knowledge, will try to cut the tumor out completely, including a small margin of good tissue all the way around the tumor. By getting a little "margin" of good tissue, they can be assured that they have removed the cancerous tumor.

Once the tumor is removed, it is immediately sent to the lab, who will analyze it to determine or verify the type of cancer and to make sure the surgeon had good margins, that the entire tumor was removed. If the lab determines that there is a section of the tumor that was cut into, indicating that the entire tumor was not removed, then a patient will go back into surgery to remove the part that may have been missed. Thus, the surgeon who is effective at getting good margins is a surgeon effective at getting the entire tumor the first time and saving you from a potential second surgery.

Now, things happen. You may have the best surgeon in the world, with an ability to get margins unlike anyone else, yet, he or she may not get yours. The tumor may have changed, parts of the tumor may not be visible during surgery; there are a variety of factors. Should the lab find that there are not clear margins, you and your surgeon will decide on next steps, such as additional surgery.

Nipples

To be perfectly honest, it didn't really occur to me that I would lose my nipples as part of the mastectomy. I knew the entire breast would be removed, but somehow, I envisioned the surgeon removing the inside of the breast, not necessarily the outside, including the nipple. Fortunately, I am one to ask many questions. So, when the surgeon described how she would do the incision, I asked if she would go around the nipple. No, she explained, because many breast cancers are ductal carcinomas, meaning that the cancer is in the milk ducts. The milk ducts all converge at the nipple, so removing the nipple is often critical in the surgery. The incisions, by the way, are made across your breast – from side to side. Somehow, I had thought they might go vertically.

The good news is that there are now some ways that nipples can be conserved; not for everyone, but for the right candidate some new and effective surgical techniques can spare the nipple. As with so much, ask your surgeon whether nipple conservation is a possibility for you.

Sentinel Node

You often hear about lymph node removal, so let's dive into this part in a little bit more detail. If a cancer from the breast metastasizes, it typically will move first into the lymph nodes located under your arms, where it then can move through your entire lymphatic system and into other parts of your body. So, an important step in your treatment is determining whether the cancer has moved into your lymph nodes as that may dictate what other courses of action are required.

Often the surgeons will remove several lymph nodes just to be sure that they have gotten any chance of the cancer's movement. However, they need to determine whether

> **Donna's Dad**
>
> *Donna's surgeon just finished and we spoke to her. She said that everything went great, and the preliminary frozen sections showed no cancer cells in the lymph nodes. So she was pleased with that. They'll have to wait for the final testing to verify that. Donna's plastic surgeon is now performing the breast reconstruction. More later.*

the cancer has moved to the lymph system or not, so they conduct a test of the "sentinel node." The sentinel nodes are the first lymph nodes that the cancer could go to from the breast. The number of sentinel nodes depends on the individual and number from 1 to 5. This test involves inserting a dye that will visually show the surgeon whether the cancer is present in the first, or sentinel, lymph nodes or not. If cancer is present, then more lymph nodes may be taken in surgery. If it is not shown in the sentinel nodes, then usually two to three lymph nodes may be removed.

Let's talk about this sentinel node test. Of all the things I had done, and I had plenty done, this is the one that bothered me the most. Before you are scared off by this, let me calm you by saying that I had a rather unique experience in that I had to have the sentinel node dye inserted right before surgery at another location from my actual surgery. So, I had to have this done and then travel across town for the double mastectomy. It is highly possible that you will be able to have the test and the surgery all in one facility, which would eliminate the unpleasantness that I experienced.

Donna

So, let's move on to the next medical topic - reconstruction. I went to the plastic surgeon on Thursday to begin to understand what that process will look like for me. Typically, people have a mastectomy and start reconstruction all at one time. We were thinking that would be an option for me. Mind you, we still don't know exactly what type of surgery I will have.

This appointment was about collecting options. Unfortunately, reconstruction at time of mastectomy (assuming that is what they do), may not be an option for me. There are really two fundamental reasons. 1. The surgeon was very concerned about all the surgery I had in the past year + or so (for my leg). To do reconstruction on top of a mastectomy adds an additional two to four hours to the surgery. She didn't think that having me under anesthesia that much after everything I have had would be wise. 2. The blood issue I have been having. My blood counts have been an issue for a bit during this chemo. She would prefer that I wait until I am fully recovered from the chemo before we do the beginning of reconstruction surgery.

Now the challenge with waiting on the reconstruction is radiation. If I have to have radiation, then the options on reconstruction are limited. I am expecting radiation after surgery but will be most thrilled if I don't have to have that. Apparently, radiation damages the skin such that it doesn't stretch anymore. That means a simple implant is not possible (unless it is done before the radiation begins, of course).

So, my option, then, if I want reconstruction, will be a procedure where they take part of my stomach or back and reconstruct with that. That type of procedure wouldn't be done for at least a year or so after I finish all treatment. They need you pretty healthy to do that type of surgery.

Next time not so technical and much more fun. But as they say....now you know the rest of the story...

Donna

The dye that will light up the sentinel nodes if cancer is present is injected into the skin around your nipple and areola. While unpleasant, that was not the worst part in my mind. The awful part? Because I was still awake and would need to move to another facility, they numbed my nipple for this injection by putting ice and freezing compresses on for around 15 minutes. I can't make this up. That ice, there, was horrible! I didn't feel the injection, so I guess it worked. But, oh my!

I realize that I have made this surgery process seem somewhat easy and straightforward. Nothing could be further from the truth. Plus, there will be so many variables thrown at you with language like margins and sentinel nodes, which are new to you, further adding to the complexity. However, at this point, I have only discussed removing the cancer. There is an entire other side to the equation: reconstructing your breast.

RECONSTRUCTION OPTIONS

As soon as you learn that you have breast cancer, you may very well begin thinking about surgical options, such as lumpectomy and mastectomy. However, many women don't realize that they can and should begin planning for reconstruction right away as well. Women I interviewed for this book shared a few reasons why they did not think about reconstruction at first. 1. Everything was so new and moving so fast that it did not occur to them. 2. They thought the cancer surgeon would just take care of the reconstruction. 3. They thought that insurance would not cover that.

Let's address these concerns. To begin with, things *are* moving fast. You hardly know which end is up as you run from doctor to doctor after diagnosis. However, when you meet with your surgical oncologist, ask him or her about reconstruction and whom they suggest you meet as a potential surgeon, usually a plastic surgeon. Quite frankly, if a surgical oncologist said he or she would reconstruct, I would raise an eyebrow and get a second opinion. There are a few surgeons who have done both breast surgery and plastic surgery fellowships, but not many.

Now, it would be great if the surgical oncologist were to suggest that you talk to a reconstruction specialist, to help get you thinking about that phase, but, that doesn't always happen. Truthfully, the surgical oncologist is concerned with your cancer and its treatment. If the doctor does not mention reconstruction, *you* should, so that you can begin to explore those options. And, yes, insurance does cover breast reconstruction, mandated to do so by federal law in 1998.

Many women think of reconstruction strictly for mastectomy patients, those who have lost the entire breast. However, even with a small tumor removed by a lumpectomy, reconstruction may be something for you to consider. Depending on the location of the tumor and size of your breast, the removal of the lump may cause your two sides to look uneven. A plastic surgeon who understands form, figure, and aesthetic can reconstruct your breast in a way that restores symmetry. Often with a mastectomy, initial reconstruction can be done at the same time. This can be less traumatic for the patient as you awake from surgery with breasts, and it saves you from being put under anesthesia any more than necessary.

Typically with a lumpectomy, surgical implants are not required for reconstruction, but other options, such as fat grafts or fat transfers, are possible. Therefore, even if you are having a small lumpectomy, consultation with a reconstruction surgeon is advantageous so that you get the best result possible. Unlike with a mastectomy, reconstruction is not generally done at the same time as a lumpectomy. Depending on your cancer and your doctor, though, exceptions exist.

Implants

The most common way to reconstruct post breast mastectomy is with implants. While this procedure is technically simple, it does typically call for several stages, or surgeries.

There are options for you, and the first stage can be done immediately with your mastectomy or delayed. The first stage includes inserting what is called an expander, which is placed either totally or partially under the muscle and filled with saline over time. The removal of the breast involves the removal of a lot of tissue, including skin. The purpose of the expander is to slowly stretch the skin so that it is ready to take on a full implant.

After this first surgery, of both a mastectomy and the initial stage of reconstruction, expect to spend a night in the hospital, waking up to a catheter, morphine, and multiple tubes to remove the fluids that may accumulate post surgery. The tubes will need to be drained every several hours, and you may have them for anywhere from one week to six weeks, depending on how you are healing. Given the tubes, the pain, the inability to use your arms, and the strong medications, you'll need to have someone available to help you for a few weeks after your surgery.

While you will follow-up with your oncology surgeon, most of your "post-op" visits will be with your reconstruction surgeon as this process continues. The stretching of the skin, to create the eventual pocket for the implant, occurs over a period of weeks and months. These appointments are typically called "fills" as the surgeon is literally filling the expander every two to three weeks or so, until you are the desired size.

These fill appointments were initially very disconcerting to me. Granted, the procedure doesn't really hurt because once you have had the mastectomy, you will have limited feeling around the breast. The disconcerting part was the size of the syringe. The first time I saw that, well, good golly, I wasn't so sure. I include a picture here, as it would have made it easier for me had I known in advance what I was going to get. But, again I say, getting the fill does not hurt, as a rule.

While getting the fill doesn't hurt, pain comes later with the stretching and pressure for which a muscle relaxer is prescribed to handle the expansion more comfortably. After a few days, the pain subsides, and about two to four weeks later, you are ready for another fill. Should you be having radiation, the fills must be completed first as radiated skin will no longer stretch.

Complications do occur with expanders. The expander can rotate, deflate, have a wrinkle or ripple in it that may require surgical intervention, and it can pop through the skin. It may be in place during radiation, and the pocket become

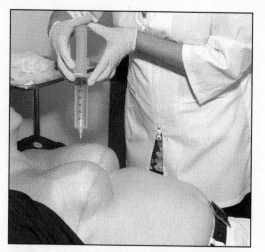

Photo courtesy of Judith Gurley MD

very tight around the expander. It is important to follow the plastic surgeon's recommendation with regard to physical and occupational therapy, massage, and range of motion.

My plastic surgeon and radiation oncologist had a number of conversations trying to determine the best route for me. The oncologist, of course, did not want to wait too long to begin radiation. The plastic surgeon knew that the best reconstruction option for me was implants, so coordinating the timing was critical.

In the end, shoulder problems following my mastectomy so limited my range of motion that I couldn't do any radiation until I got the full movement of my arms back. (My arms had to be over my head for extended periods of time to receive the radiation.) This delay allowed for plenty of time to get the expanders fully – well - expanded.

Donna

The good news here, I do NOT need shoulder surgery. What? You are all saying. Yep, that has been the concern this week. Off and on I have mentioned this shoulder and how sore it is. The fact of the matter is I can hardly hold a coffee cup in my right hand because of the shoulder pain.

The plastic surgeon and radiation oncologist were very concerned. The pain keeps me up most of the night (typical of shoulder problems). However, I need to be able to sleep if I am going to have radiation, or I won't be able to get through it. Because the pain has not improved since the mastectomy, there was concern that a surgical fix might be required. (This shoulder issue is from the mastectomy. They kept this arm in an awkward position for a number of hours, and things like this are common after that type of surgery.)

So, I learned yesterday at the orthopedist that the shoulder is impinged, and I have rotator cuff tendonitis and bursitis, neither of which needs to be fixed surgically. The best option would be an anti-inflammatory medication. However, with my still low blood counts, they can't give me an anti-inflammatory. So, right now they have me on a bit of Vicodin to manage the pain. We will check next week with the oncology team to see if I can receive a cortisone shot in my shoulder, as that would manage the pain and allow me to get through radiation.

The second stage of reconstruction is the insertion of the implants. No, you cannot live with expanders forever! I asked. In fact, my doctor was surprised I asked as most women can't wait to get the expanders out. Implants are designed to stay in for years and years, so the critical next step is to put the implants in place. Of course, there continue to be timing considerations. I could not have surgery to place the implants until six months after my radiation was completed because the body needs that much time to heal before the trauma of additional surgery, or your results and, in fact, your health may be risk.

If you are not receiving radiation, the earliest expanders can come out and the permanent implant inserted is three months. Expanders can stay in up to a year or two; however, they have a high rupture rate, so this is not recommended. They are considered temporary devices.

Insertion of implants is not as major as the initial mastectomy and expander surgery. It can even be done on an outpatient basis in some situations. Still, you will return home with medications for the pain. If possible, the surgeons will use the scar from the previous surgery for the incision, so you will not have a new scar. You may return home with a tube or two for any fluid drainage, and you will need some down time for recovery. While your chest will be sore, usually, the surgeon does not need to cut the chest muscle, just move it around a bit. So, while there is pain, it is not like the massive surgery you had with the mastectomy and expanders. A little point to note is that often the final implant is sewn into your chest with dissolving stitches. About three months after my implant was inserted, I found a red zigzag line across the scar where the implant was. Concerned, I contacted the doctor and discovered that as the stitches dissolve, they sometimes work their way to the surface and can be seen through the thin skin layer as a red zigzag. In another six to nine months, they may fully dissolve so that you will no longer see them.

The implants as they are put in will be your final size. Yes, you can choose your size, but with some restrictions, typically due to the quality and thickness of the overlying muscle and skin. You want to avoid over stretching or over thinning these tissues. Some women choose to go up or down in size. Working with your plastic surgeon, you can determine the right size for you.

While nipple conservation is now sometimes a possibility, more often it requires a third stage of reconstruction. A very simple way of reconstructing the nipple is to tattoo it on. Again, your plastic surgeon is the one to speak with about this, not a tattoo shop! Your plastic surgeon may refer you to a tattoo artist if you're interested in getting a 3-D nipple tattoo, but start with you plastic surgeon, not the artist!

To truly recreate a nipple, the plastic surgeon can remove a little skin from your bikini line, tattoo that skin in the appropriate color, and reconstruct the shape of the nipple. While you will not necessarily get sensation back into your nipples, you will get the more natural breast form as a result. A word to the wise: When I first heard about nipple reconstruction, well meaning friends familiar with reconstruction insights from a few years earlier told me that the skin was removed from "down there" as that skin is very similar to normal nipple skin. No way Jose was I going that route. Turns out that type of reconstruction is outdated and not commonly done anymore. In the course of talking about it with plastic surgeons, I learned that there have been some advances that make nipple reconstruction quite effective and tolerable. So, don't hesitate to ask your plastic surgeon how he or she suggests you reconstruct your nipples.

Tram And Diep Flap

Another procedure other than implants that can be used to reconstruct your breasts is called the tram flap. In this procedure the skin and tissue are taken from another part of the body, typically your back, abdomen, or buttock muscles, to create a new breast. In this procedure, the transplanted tissue must be reattached to the blood vessels of the new chest area. It is a difficult procedure for both doctor and patient. While it was common many years ago, many doctors and facilities no longer perform it due to the numerous risks, complications, and the very difficult recovery for patients.

The DIEP flap uses the woman's own abdominal skin and fat to recreate the breast. Significantly, this procedure preserves all the abdominal muscles, meaning the patient has less pain and a faster recovery. As with the Tram flap, micro surgery is required to connect the blood vessels. While this option is much preferable to the Tram flap, it does require a highly skilled and trained micro-vascular plastic surgeon.

COMPLICATIONS

Complications are a significant concern any time you have surgery, and they certainly are for the breast cancer patient. Infection leads the list of complications that are very concerning, so your surgeons may often prescribe an antibiotic to help prevent infection from setting in. Should you have infection indications, such as red streaks or fever, be sure to alert your doctor. Infections not treated may require additional surgeries or other more serious interventions.

Another common complication is limited mobility as the scar tissue forms. The surgeon may recommend physical and occupational therapy in order to get back to full range of motion. A more significant complication from surgery is lymphodema, which results when the lymphatic system is damaged. This topic is discussed in great detail in the chapter Burn, Burn, Burn as it is often a complication of radiation as well.

Sometimes getting the aesthetic right can take a few tries. While not a complication per se, the surgeon may need to "go back in" to correct the look as your body heals. In my case, the expanders moved up closer to my shoulders after they were first inserted. While I joked that I now had really perky girls, the fact of the matter was, additional surgery was required to bring them back into place. As I healed and the expanders settled down, a flap of skin developed under both breasts, so additional surgery was required to clean that up.

AESTHETICS AND SYMMETRY

A very important reason to go to a plastic surgeon for your reconstruction is that he or she will have a strong aesthetic sense, understanding, at its core, the human form, proportions, and what is pleasing to the human eye. In reconstructing your breast(s), he or she will take into consideration symmetry, evenness, location on your chest, and size that will balance and be in proportion to your body.

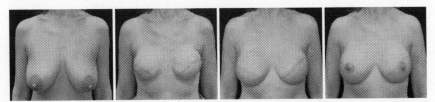

Photos courtesy of Judith Gurley MD

A good plastic surgeon will share reconstruction photos of former patients, with their faces always hidden. When photos were first shared with me, I didn't know what I was looking for, but, soon, I was able to discern when breasts were uneven or asymmetrical. I began to look for surgeons who were great surgeons, doctors, but who also had a strong sense of aesthetics and beauty.

The thing to realize is that doctors who are good at their craft and have a great eye for aesthetics will want to make sure that they have reconstructed you as beautifully as possible. To that end, there may be little "tweaks" that they want to make to ensure that you have the best and most physically appealing result. This is especially true as you heal and your body settles in to its new shape. Skin may sag, expanders may move, all sorts of things can happen as you heal. Keep in mind that a little tweak is still additional anesthetic and surgery to you. Despite that, follow their advice. You have come this far, your cancer is removed, and you can have a beautiful chest again.

FASHION, FOOD, FATIGUE

WARDROBE FOR THE CANCER JOURNEY

Ordinarily, I like any opportunity to shop, though I have to admit,
I would have much preferred not having to shop because of cancer.
First, I was pretty tired, and shopping, while fun, really exhausted me.
Second, the whole I was shopping for items *because* I had cancer bit.
The challenge, I found, is that I really didn't know what I was going to
need until right before I had to get it, or sometimes even after the fact.
My hope here is that I can save you from the aggravation and energy
expenditure of fast trips to the store or expensive overnight shipping
charges by providing you with a sense of what to look for in advance.

Chemo Clothes

There is a lot to think
about when it comes
to comfortable, and,
yes, stylish clothes,
to wear while you are
going through chemo,

> **Donna**
> *Meanwhile, as one last fun thing before my second
> chemo, Mom and I took a stroll through the St.
> Louis Art Fair, and lo and behold, they had a
> hat artist! Were we in heaven or what? We tried
> on hats, and I found a lovely soft gray felt one
> that should do the trick on a cold fall day. I hope
> everyone had a lovely weekend as well....*

beginning with what to wear to receive your chemo. Not that you
have to be glamorous, mind you. If you have a long day of treatment,
you want something comfortable. While many women wear sweats
to chemo, I am not really a sweatsuit/ sweatshirt type of gal, so I
found some other options. To be honest, I did get a little dressed up. I
always feel more in control when I am "dressed."

One consideration in dressing for your day of chemo is where your
port is located. Typically it is in your upper chest and neck. I made the

mistake of wearing a turtleneck once. While the nurses could access the port, it did stretch the turtleneck, and, more importantly, pulled on the port while I received the chemo, which was a bit uncomfortable. A knit v-neck, round, or boatneck shirt is a comfortable and easy port access option. Wearing layers like a knit shirt with a jacket or sweater (again with a round or v-neck collar) made port access easy and kept me warm. Avoid white or light colors, though. While the nurses are spectacular at accessing the port with minimal bleeding, it can still happen, and no need ruining a white shirt.

Another consideration for chemo day is the pants you wear. This is not really the time to wear your cute skinny jeans. As part of chemo, a lot of fluids are pushed into you. As a result, you may feel bloated and will probably make many trips to the restroom. So, relaxed pants or skirts that expand a little as you take in the fluids will make that experience more comfortable. I found that leggings with a long knit jacket over a t-shirt worked well for me: easy port access, comfortable as the fluids flowed in, somewhat stylish, and warm.

Speaking of warm, you might want to consider bringing your own soft blanket, pashmina, or wrap to chemo. While plenty of blankets are available on site, they just seem so medicinal and not at all cozy. Sitting all day, receiving chemo, you may get cold. You may also experience hot flashes, so having something you can throw on and off easily is a plus.

Getting through your chemo is just one part of the story, however. The real challenge occurs when you are at home, at work, living your everyday life. You will likely feel quite fatigued and in need of naps during the day. Finding clothes that are comfortable and do not wrinkle should a nap be required makes getting through the day away from home a little easier. One friend mentioned that she went to work every day through her cancer without telling a soul that she was sick. She scheduled "meetings" in the afternoon for napping purposes; she would lock her office door, lie on the couch, and take a little nap. Finding clothes that didn't wrinkle and that allowed her to go on to her next meeting feeling put together was key for her.

Knit clothing can be a great option during chemo. It can be very soft, doesn't wrinkle badly should a nap be required, and can be quite stylish. While I was working and going through chemo, I became a fan of Misook clothing. Knit-like, it is light weight (as even heavy clothes felt burdensome to me), fashionable, and good for the office, and a few pieces went a long way. Once I found some knit t-shirts that I liked, I bought them in a variety of colors. Mixing and matching different color tees with scarves to cover the port, I was able to go to work stylishly but comfortably, and no one was the wiser.

> **Donna**
>
> *The question of the day is, what exactly constitutes "therapy"? See, I believe my oncologist said I was to stay in and rest except for my therapy appointments.*
>
> *So when my car ended up at at the mall, and I ended up shopping for shoes, I figured that was fine as it was mental or emotional (or both) therapy for me!*
>
> *And, they brought the shoes to me! So, no physical stress at all. Now, my physical therapist for my leg insists that the oncologist could not possibly have meant anything but strict physical therapy.*
>
> *But, please, a woman who has had nine surgeries in less than two years can't exist without a little shoe therapy - don't you think? To top it off, four pair of the cutest flat shoes, with rubber soles! Did you know Chanel even makes cute flats with rubber soles? I mean, how else are you going to learn if you don't look at them live? And they are cute!*
>
> *This was awesome therapy!!!*

Another important consideration for your clothing choices is your skin. As I discuss in the Dry, Dry, Dry chapter, your skin will be uncomfortably dry and very sensitive. So, fabric choices and styles may concern you more now than ever before. As a result, you want to invest in a few pieces that are really soft and comfortable. Wearing knit t-shirts underneath longer knit jackets or sweaters can look casually chic while preventing irritation to your skin. If you find sweaters to be too itchy, consider cashmere, and if you are going to invest in a more expensive sweater, like a cashmere one, consider getting a button-down. Even if it is not your usual style, it may be more practical depending on the other treatments you receive and your ability to move your arms and/ or chest and back.

Another clothing consideration is that your chemo and many of your medications may give you hot flashes. So, fabrics made of natural fibers and that breathe may be more comfortable for you, as well clothes that can be easily layered. Cotton knits fit the bill for many women in that they are soft, drape nicely, can be layered, and breathe fairly well.

Both brick and mortar and online stores offer comfortable knit clothing that looks as great as it feels. My favorite go to clothing lines were Eileen Fisher and Soft Surroundings, both of which carry longer button down tunics, jackets, and knit pants. Eileen Fisher can be found in a variety of department stores, their own shops, and online. Soft Surroundings is a growing chain that specializes in fashionable, soft, comfortable products. While their stores are not everywhere yet, their clothes can be found online as well. Soft Surroundings identifies the level of softness for most of their items, which can aid you in finding things that are really comfortable for your needs.

SURGERY

Many times surgery is an important part of your treatment, and when it is, it will impact the way you dress. First, your movement will be limited. Second, the doctor may want compression around the surgical site. These two considerations, while critical for your recovery, may direct the type of clothes that you can and should wear.

Should you have to have upper body surgery, know that your arm movement may be greatly restricted, that you may not be able to get your arms over your head. Clothing that buttons or zippers up the front will be easier for you to get on and off. As I mention in the chemo section, knit products are great for their comfort. Additionally, they do stretch a little if you really have to put something on over your head. Also, realize that you also need to be able to dress your lower body. Don't try to deal with those tight jeans when your arms have restricted movement. Stretch, knit pants will be easier to pull on. Also, slip on, flat shoes are best. Slip on, as it will be hard to bend down and tie or buckle shoes; flat because you can't use your arms to catch yourself should you start to fall. In all seriousness, wear the flat shoes! You may very likely be on pain medicine, which can make you groggy, and without your arms to catch you, just a little slip, and you may have other issues. Be safe on this one. For dressier occasions, consider investing in a cape or two. A cape is easy to put on over a knit shirt and can look very chic and put together, even with limited arm movements.

Another consideration is that with arm restrictions, you may only be able to lift a few pounds post surgery. I don't know about you, but my purses can hit the five to eight pound level if I am not careful. So, make sure you have a little bag available that you can put your essentials into: lipstick, pain medication, credit card, phone, etc. Depending on your surgery, a shoulder bag may not work as it can hit the tubes, and it may irritate the shoulder. A little casual clutch may serve you very well for any trips you take out of the house post surgery.

I mention tubes, a big consideration for surgical patients. After a major operation like mastectomy, lung, or colon surgery, you will likely awaken with multiple drainage tubes coming out of you. These tubes are usually long with a bulb at the end to collect the fluids that may be accumulating, so that the fluids are moved out of your body. These tubes can be pinned to your clothes or to a wrap around your waist. Of course you will want to keep these hidden and under your clothes. Again, long knit-like jackets and sweaters can serve you well to hide the tubes as well as the extra "girth" they provide.

Coming out of my double mastectomy, I had six total tubes, three on each side. It took between six to eight weeks before all of my tubes were removed. So, having clothes that worked for the tubes was important during that entire period. In preparing you for surgery, the hospital will tell you to arrive with loose and comfortable clothing for returning home. Between the possibility of tubes and limited movement, that is great advice.

Compression is another important aspect of recovery. Typically, the doctors will send you home with compression garments that are

> **Donna**
>
> *Ahhhhh, the simple pleasure of a shower!*
>
> *When I finally took a shower, it was great. It was just the hour or so of preparation that was the drag. Oh, it doesn't take you an hour? Well, let me explain my process.*
>
> *First, get all potentially necessary items on small sink counter. Second, drain all tubes and record results. Third, remove gauze around tubes. (Not usually difficult, but the tubes are on my side almost under my arms, and my arms don't like to reach up yet.) Fourth, reattach tubes to special belt just for showering. Fifth, shower- YEAH! Sixth, unattach all tubes, dry off, including all tubes. Seventh, put on medication and gauze pads. Eighth, reattach tubes to clothes. Ninth, get dressed. Tenth, rest for another hour after all that!!*

to be worn round the clock and designed so you are able to put them on without pulling on the incisions. As you recover, the doctors may release you to wear other compression garments (such as Spanx or fitted camis) in place of strictly medical ones. On this topic, you need to talk to your own doctors who have seen what works and will have strong opinions on what they want you to wear. In your pre-surgical consults, ask what they advise you to wear so that if you need to purchase something new, you can do that in advance.

If your surgery is more in your lower body, the same issues will apply. You may want to have some long, flowing shirts, sweaters, or jackets to cover the tubes.

Whatever the surgery, be cautious as you get dressed so that you are not pulling your incisions. Know that you will rest, rest, rest, so comfortable

Donna

In the spirit of St. Valentine's Day - lots of LOVE to each and every one of you! I am feeling better, although as Mom might attest, I am very poor company as I do, really, sleep constantly!

Yesterday, however, I was feeling a tad bit better and suggested that we go out to a store or do something that Mom wanted to do. We went to the Gifted Gardener, one of my favorite little stores here. Yes, Karen and Jen, I finally took Mom there. After finding some fun things, we thought some lunch would perk me up because, you see, I was fading already. So, it was off to Oceana's, one of Mom's favorite restaurants in town, for a bite. Then we went to Soft Surroundings, another of her favorite stores. Well, she found some lovely clothes, so it was a very successful trip.

However, may I point out that my definition of a "little" shopping trip has changed. How do I know this? I went home and slept something like four hours to recuperate. Importantly, I didn't buy one thing at Soft Surroundings, probably an historic event to be recorded. You see, I was too tired to even to look, let alone try on. Ah well. All was fun, and nurse Mom needed a day out!!!

Now, for the really big news! The tubes came out this week! I cannot begin to tell you what a pain those things are. I've been trying to come up with songs to summarize this most exceptional turn of events. Let me try a few on you....

TUBE FREE....as free as the wind blows. As free as the grass grows....

OR:

Ding dong the tubes are gone, yucky tubes, nasty tubes, ding dong the wicked tubes are gone....

OR:

Tubey, tubey, tube..... (As Frank Sinatra sings).

clothes that go on easily and that you can sleep in are key. Wear something that works for the entire day, as fatigue may limit your interest in dressing for different activities as the day progresses. The picture seems a little bleak right now, but remember, as my brother-in-law reminded me, the spectacular thing about bodies is that they heal. And yours will too. Just give it time.

RADIATION

Radiation provides a few different clothing considerations. The primary concern is the radiation burn. Identifying clothing items that are very soft and comfortable on radiated skin is critical. Again, very soft, cotton t-shirts are a good option. Rather than suddenly, radiation burn typically develops over time, and so, as you start feeling your clothes begin to irritate your skin, switch to the softer, comfortable knits I talk about. You may also find that you need to dress your radiation burns (discussed in the Burn, Burn, Burn chapter). So, loose, comfortable clothes that allow for dressings, bandages, and gauze underneath are your best option.

I found some inexpensive, nice looking polyester blend t-shirts in a variety of colors that worked perfectly for radiation as I could wear them under my work suits. Part of why they worked well is that they were tighter, offering some compression versus a typical cotton tee. Additionally, I used a lot of Aquaphor on my radiated skin, and it easily washed out of the shirts. Because they were really smooth, and soft, they were comfortable as the treatment progressed and my skin became pink and then red.

If you are having surgery followed by radiation, discuss the compression garments you will be wearing with your doctors. The surgeon will need you in compression garments to ensure healing and a good result. The radiation oncologist can help you determine the best way to protect your radiated skin while wearing the compression garment. Also, you may find a few range of motions issues as your radiated area becomes tender and sore. So, the comfortable, free swinging, easy to put on knits discussed earlier may be the best clothing choice during radiation as well.

SIZING

No one told me that my clothing sizes might change during the various surgeries and treatments. Truth be told, I didn't spend much time asking or thinking about it. However, do be aware that the various treatments can impact your size. For instance, chemo and the associated steroids can really bloat you or make you puffy. People talk about being on the "chemo diet" because you often do not feel like eating, but, in fact, you may not lose weight because of the medicines you are on.

Should you be going through a mastectomy or double mastectomy, you will find your top half to be a different size post surgery. I had to purchase some tight fitting tank tops for compression after my double mastectomy. I bought them in my pre-surgery size, but because I dropped more than one size, the tanks no longer offered the compression I needed at the time. I learned later that the doctors could have offered some advice on the change in size because of the work they were going to do. Again, something like this is not a huge deal; however, I just don't think you should have to go shopping again, especially when you are exhausted and recuperating post surgery. A little information, so that you ask your doctors the right questions, may help you avoid extra expense and fatigue.

BRAS AND BATHING SUITS

If you are dealing with breast cancer, your bra and your bathing suit needs will change. The good news is that there is a myriad of resources available to help you find the appropriate item for the various stages of your treatments and life after treatment.

Again, your doctor will have strong opinions on what you should wear, so make sure you ask him or her. The bra becomes a very important garment during the mastectomy and lumpectomy as it allows for improved support and compression that will aid in healing. It is an important garment for radiation as well, especially in terms of treating your sensitive skin with care. Your bra will not necessarily play a factor in your chemo, as the chemo impacts your entire body, not just your breast.

Typically, you will be advised to stay away from underwire bras. They are not advisable after mastectomy or lumpectomy surgeries until okayed by the doctor. My doctors did not want me to wear any underwire product until my expanders had been removed and my final implants inserted. Additionally, underwire garments may be very uncomfortable should you be getting radiation as they may just further irritate your skin.

As you move past all your treatments, your doctors will advise when you can move back to more normal bras, including the underwire ones. You may want to go to a department store, a bra shop, or a medical supply store that provides post-mastectomy products to be properly fitted for a bra once you are able to return to normal garments. Most likely your size will have changed and an expert in fitting bras can help you find the product that works best and is most comfortable for you. Also, realize that you may be able to return to a normal bra before your nipples are reconstructed. Again, bra fitters will be able to identify garments that will be smooth and shapely, even if you don't have nipples yet.

Should you have decided to have a mastectomy or double mastectomy and *not* have reconstruction, there are many types of prosthesis that you can put into your bras, or that are designed into the bra, itself, to provide you the shape of having your full breasts. For these types of products, look for specialty bra shops or medical supply stores that have mastectomy sections. The people that work in these stores are experts at assisting you to create the smooth shape you seek. While you can also order these products online, for the first time or two, a store visit will help you understand the various materials, costs, and feel of the options available.

As you go through treatments, you will be encouraged to be active as that can help with your fatigue. For many, that may be swimming. Be sure to check with your doctor, though, regarding when you can get into a chlorinated pool after surgery or whether you can get in at all during radiation. The chlorine may really irritate that radiated area, so check first.

In general, bathing suit decisions during treatment follow many of the same recommendations for selecting bras. Stay away from underwire ones post surgery. Many of the same bra shops and medical supply stores will offer mastectomy swimming suit options along with the bras. So, that is a great place to start. If you opted for reconstruction, you may want to look for bathing suits with more chest and side coverage in order to hide the surgical scars. If you decided on using prosthesis instead of reconstruction, you can find bathing suits with spaces in which your prosthesis can sit, providing you with a shapely form as a result. Again, starting with a specialty store that provides this type of swimming suit can be helpful as you learn what will work best for you and your surgeries. As you become comfortable with what you personally prefer, you will find various options. For example, companies like Lands' End now provide an array of mastectomy styled bathing suits. Remember that your skin will be very sensitive to the sun from radiation as well as the many medications you are taking. So, regardless of the bathing suit you get, don't forget the sunscreen!

As a quick summary, post surgery you will be in tighter compression garments. Should you have expanders and then reconstruction, form fitting, high control camisoles or tanks may be needed. For radiation, a control bra without a wire may be required. All of these variations are used to help ensure appropriate healing and minimal irritation as you recover from your surgeries and radiation. But, fundamentally, work with your doctor on what under garments to wear as he or she knows what will help to ensure a good recovery and outcome for you.

FOOD

Let's start this chapter by acknowledging that it is not called nutrition. It is not called diet. I am not a nutritionist, I am not a dietician. There are many great books out there on nutrition and diets for the cancer patient. However, you do need to eat even when you don't feel like it. You need to fuel your body as you go through your treatments, so in this chapter, I share some of the tips and tricks discovered to make your food more palatable.

Food As Fuel

Many of us eat for taste as well as to fuel our bodies. However, as you go through your cancer treatments, your focus must be

> **Donna**
> *Phewww....the Mac Truck seems to be headed out of town. Feeling much better today - YEAH. The food conundrum is an interesting combination of not wanting food and not keeping any of the food forced in, in me. Don't worry Mom... and Dad....and Karen.... and Jen...and.....well everyone.... I am eating as much as I can as I know I have to to fight this Cancer. (Side note - from now on, Cancer will be spelled with little "c". Let's not give it too much credit! :)).*

on fueling your body. Much like your car needs gasoline to move, you need food (your fuel) to move. Unfortunately, your willingness and ability to eat may dramatically change as you go through your cancer treatments. If you don't get enough of the right kind of fuel for your body, the cancer treatments become even more difficult. Eating well and eating enough can help with everything from withstanding side effects to healing and recovering more quickly to lowering your risk of infection to simply feeling better and stronger.

Eating well means providing the nutrients, such as protein, carbohydrates, fats, water, vitamins, and minerals that your body needs to stay healthy while you fight your cancer. However, depending on the kind of cancer you have, you may be advised to avoid certain things, such as fiber. When you layer on the change in your sense of taste, the fatigue, and other side effects, eating a balanced diet that nourishes your body becomes more and more challenging.

Taste Change

Things that typically are very appealing may not taste good to you at all while you are receiving treatment. Conversely, foods you have never cared for before may actually taste good, so this becomes a great time to try new foods. Commonly people experience a metallic taste in part as a result of changes to their salivary glands. One way to minimize the metallic taste is to eat with *plastic* utensils instead of using silverware.

Another way to manage taste is to try to eat foods frozen or at room temperature. Let your hot foods cool down a bit, before you eat them. For instance, even chicken noodle soup was more appealing to me when it was warm rather than hot. By serving food in this manner, you can decrease the taste of the food as well as the smells associated with it. I was

> **Donna**
>
> *I am tired a bit more today, and my tastes they are a-changing again. Boo hoo...Mom is preparing a lovely salmon dish tonight, and I am so hoping I can fully enjoy it! I'll let you know tomorrow. Please keep your fingers crossed that I can taste it still!*
>
> **Donna – Next Morning**
>
> *A morning update! First off, the salmon was delicious, as was the curry rice. The bad news was, once again, the first taste to go has been that for white wine. You know how I love a glass of pinot grigio.* ☹

advised to freeze fruits for snacking. My sister took that idea to heart and froze grapes, blueberries, sliced watermelon, and pineapple. While the frozen grapes were the only item I ate with any consistency, many other chemo patients swear by the frozen fruit idea, so certainly give it a try. Another remedy for metallic tastes is tart or sour foods, such as citrus fruits, pickles, lemonade, and cranberry juices.

You may find while you undergo chemo that meat does not taste good. Substitute other high protein foods, such as milk, yogurt, cheese, beans, and eggs. Marinating meat, poultry, and fish in sweet sauces, such as sweet wine, salad dressing, or even fruit juices can cut the metallic and poor taste of foods.

If none of these strategies works, cleansing your palate by rinsing your mouth with tea or ginger ale, salt water or water with baking soda, before eating may do the trick. And for between meals, peppermints, lemon drops, and gum can keep a sweet taste in your mouth while preventing it from becoming too dry.

WATER, WATER, WATER

Staying hydrated is one of the simplest and best things you can do for yourself. Water and other fluids are vital for your health for a number of reasons. To begin with, your body is composed of about 60 percent water. That water is critical for your circulation, digestion, absorption, saliva production, and nutrient transportation, to name a few functions. These systems are already taxed by your treatments, so, you don't want to exacerbate the situation by limiting your fluid intake as well.

Water is also important in energizing your muscles. On a basic level, we know this from all the sports drinks advertising. But, realize that as you undergo treatment, your muscles may get sore from medications. Or, they may simply fall prey to fatigue. Water and other healthy fluids can help your muscles' cells to rebuild and your muscles recover more fully.

Specifically while you undergo chemo, you will find that the more water and fluids you drink, the better you may actually handle your treatment. You want the chemo to go in, do its job, and get the heck out. Drinking plenty of fluids will help your kidneys flush that chemo through. By the way, the common rule of thumb is that the best fluids include anything you can see through, such as water, apple juice, gelatin, clear soup, etc., excluding alcoholic beverages.

Another point that bears repeating is that while your chemo is destroying your fast growing cancer cells, it is killing other cells as well, leading to side effects like the loss of hair and dry skin. It is difficult for your cells to rebuild themselves without plenty of water. So, fluids are critical for both maximizing the effectiveness of chemo while minimizing its side effects.

While it seems like easy advice - just drink your water - actually doing it when you are feeling ill is another story. When you are fatigued and not feeling well, everything just seems like a chore, even something simple like getting up and pouring yourself a glass of water. So, save your energy for getting that drink of water, not doing your dishes or any other task that you see. To make sure you are drinking fluids, find some things you like such as apple juice or a flavored water that you are willing to drink. Popsicles, an alternative fluid, and cold drinks may taste better, and so you may be more willing to finish them.

Consider putting berries or herbs in a pitcher of water. Rosemary especially has helpful anti-cancer properties and makes the water very refreshing. But, experiment to see what berries or herbs taste good to you during treatment. Should you be chilled and looking for a hot drink, try hot water with lemon if tea is not tasting good to you. The bonus: lemon can mitigate the metallic taste.

Speaking of heat, many ladies have horrible hot flashes as they undergo chemo, depending on the type of chemo they have. If you have hot flashes and are sweating a lot, double up on the water to counter this added loss of fluids. Additionally, digestive problems from vomiting to diarrhea can cause dehydration and loss of electrolytes. Pedialyte drinks and popsicles can help to maintain the balance your body needs. As with all others, if these side effects continue to be a problem, be sure to discuss them with your doctor as he or she can help you determine how much fluid you might need to take in during the day to compensate for what your body is losing.

SUPPLEMENTS

As soon as you hear you have cancer, you may rush to do "healthy" things, like begin to take or take more nutritional supplements. Whatever you do, talk to your doctor first. I, and others I know, were advised to stop all vitamins and supplements in case they were contributing to the cancer's growth. Depending on your cancer and treatment protocol, your doctor may be fine with the supplements. However, it is important that he or she knows what you are on in order to make that determination.

Along the same line, some supplements can help with the side effects that you experience both during and after your treatments, like nutritional shakes that are designed for people who, for a variety of reasons, are not eating well. Boost and Ensure are two such products. You may have to experiment before you find the right product for you, though. While I was on chemo, these tasted absolutely horrible to me. People stopped buying them once they realized that I was throwing out the entire can each time one was opened. Now, that doesn't mean they will taste bad to you, and if one product doesn't work, switch brands and flavors to find one that does. I did discover a product called NutraPrime. It is a shake in several

> **Judy**
> Some of my strange food issues included weight gain and craving foods that I never liked before!

flavors developed specifically for cancer patients, and designed to be easily digested and to taste good to cancer patients. The ingredients were modified to address the kind of taste changes people with cancer often experience.

In the interest of full disclosure, I will tell you that I lived across the street from a friend who was part of the team developing this product. After one of my trips to the ER, my friend brought me several bags of it. It was still in development, and I served as a bit of a test case. The good news is, it really worked. It was one of the few foods that I not only ate, but enjoyed as well. As of this writing, the company continues to build distribution of the product.

> **Donna**
> Mom and I almost got into world war three over double stuff Oreo cookies! Now the fact that they got in the house is an entirely different story. But they are here - Yeah! So, mom plans on bringing me one cookie (sigh.....). But, in a fortunate turn of events, she came to me for help in opening the package. With deft hands, I quickly grabbed three cookies. She was aghast!
>
> She decided that in the future, I need to eat a Brussels sprout for each Oreo I get. That is SO NOT happening!!
>
> Not to worry. Oreo negotiations will continue tomorrow. Indulge your sweet tooth everyone!
>
> With love,

You can find it primarily in oncology offices so far, if you want to give it a try.

It probably goes without saying, but check with your doctor on all of these products, including items like Ensure and Boost. As these supplemental drinks are made with a variety of ingredients, your doctor may have a strong opinion on what to recommend for you. And remembering that your tastes have changed, be open to the possibility that the things you didn't care for in the past may actually taste good. For instance, even if you've always avoided strawberry, that may be the one flavor that tastes best through treatment. I offer this as you don't want your pre-cancer tastes to cause you to avoid products that perhaps may taste very good to you now. And again, now might be the perfect time to try some new foods.

Organic

I am not a "foodie," and I am not an expert on the organic food perspective. However, I can offer you a few observations. First of all, once I was diagnosed, everyone from doctors to nurses to others who have had cancer told me to go organic. In fact, a nutritionist I visited explained that there is speculation that the increase in cancers we are seeing is directly related to all the hormone-fed livestock we eat. The chicken, beef, milk you eat or drink may be carrying the hormones from that source animal, and that could be stimulating cancer growth. Is this definitely true? I don't know. Is it possible? Yes.

Another controversial issue is soy. Whether speaking to doctors, chemo nurses, nutritionists, or others with cancer, I was continually told to avoid soy since I had cancer, that soy consumption might increase my chances of having a recurrence of cancer. There are several challenges with soy, a critical one being that some research shows that it is a plant-based estrogen product. There is strong evidence that links estrogen to hormonally sensitive cancers in women. To be on the safe side, I was told to avoid it. However, an equally strong argument is made on the other side of soy. Proponents of its consumption (or that one at least need not avoid soy) point to research that says the connection between soy and cancer has not been established. They point to countries like Japan that have a low rate of breast cancer but high soy consumption.

It is not all that uncommon to find differing opinions in science and medicine. As research evolves and findings change, doctors shift their recommendations. My perspective, trust your doctors. They will be trying to stay up on the latest research and recommendations. Additionally, they understand your unique situation and can advise you best in the soy – no soy debate.

So, what should you eat? Eat your vegetables and fruits that are organic as they have not been sprayed with chemicals to kill weeds, etc. Eat eggs, meat, poultry, and fish that are antibiotic and hormone free. In fish this may be labeled as "wild"; in everything else, it may be called "free range."

Within these parameters, find foods you'll like well enough to eat. And keep things as basic or simple as possible, foods that will help get the nutrients you need into your body without the additives and processed products that are not providing much nutritional value. Research supports that a healthy diet and exercise reduce the rates of recurrence of cancers.

CHEMO DIET AND DIETS FOR CHEMO

When I found out I had cancer, I looked for any silver linings in the diagnosis. One I thought of was the "chemo diet." Yeah! I might finally get skinny. If you think like I do, unfortunately, I have bad news. Weight loss does not happen very often. With the exception of some digestive cancers, such as colon, the chemo therapies and steroids often make you bloated and puffy, and so it seems like you are putting on weight. Speaking of weight, be prepared to step on a scale every single time you go to an oncology visit. Your weight change, either up or down, will be a key factor that is watched by your medical team. In fact, so many times I would "weigh in" for my oncologist, only to turn around a half hour later and "weigh in" again for the infusion room. Could it really have changed so quickly, I would ask? No, but there is no messing around with weight changes during chemo especially.

While there may not be a "chemo diet," there are diets for when you are on chemo or have cancer. I was advised early on to visit with a dietician or nutritionist. I found this to be extremely helpful and recommend that if you have been diagnosed with cancer that you do the same.

A nutritionist can help you with a number of things. He or she can consider your exact type of cancer and offer suggestions of what might be appropriate specifically for you and your situation. I was surprised to learn that food recommendations can be specific to the type of cancer you have. For instance, given the HER2 type of cancer I had, I was advised to eat more of the spice turmeric, as some research showed turmeric having anti-cancer effects. Many other herbs and supplements can also be beneficial for different cancers. Again, it is most important that you discuss this with your doctor as each person and her needs are different, and your physician can help you find the right answers for you.

Your oncology team may have a nutritionist on staff or someone that they recommend. Cancer Support Communities and Gilda's Clubs often have nutritionists available to you for consultation at no cost.

If you take anything away from this chapter, remember to eat. Well, and drink water. Not that it is easy as you go through treatment, but it is critical if you are going to have the successful treatment results you want and deserve.

I AM SOOOO TIRED... ENERGY AND FATIGUE

You often hear about fatigue, but boy is fatigue tough to explain or describe. It is so much deeper, so all encompassing, versus just being tired. Fatigue - feeling physically, mentally, and emotionally drained - is a very common side effect of cancer treatments. Whether you are receiving chemo or radiation or having surgery, fatigue can easily occur. Simply sleeping more will not necessarily reduce the fatigue.

> **Donna**
> *Key learning, my tough days post chemo are days 5 and 6. What a rough two days it has been. It feels like I have been hit by a Mack Truck. ☺ But, if all goes according to plan, I should be back in the saddle tomorrow or Monday - with bells on again may I add!!*
>
> *Happy Saturday!*

I described my fatigue as feeling like I had been hit by a Mack Truck, as it felt as if a truck had just steamrolled over me and pushed all the energy and life right out of me. Others describe fatigue as feeling tired or weak or exhausted or heavy or worn-out. It is truly all of these, though, of course, different for every person and at various stages of illness and treatment. For many going through cancer treatments, fatigue may be one of the worst side effects. Knowing that fatigue will likely happen, you can take steps to manage it and continue to live like a lady, as radiantly as that fatigue will allow.

Causes Of Fatigue

Many things may cause fatigue. First and foremost, the cancer, itself, will tax your energy. Chemo and radiation treatments, surgery, medications, not drinking enough fluids, not eating enough, infections, and side effects from treatments can also all contribute to fatigue. Your emotional state, such as feeling anxious or depressed, can be both a cause and an effect of fatigue.

How do you know if you have fatigue or are just tired? Do you feel tired even after sleeping or simply feel like you have no

> **Donna**
>
> *So, if Mack truck is the brand, then steamroller is the truck model! Wow was I slammed, steamrolled, smothered yesterday! 8 a.m. wake up. First nap from 8:30 a.m. until 11:30 a.m. Quick visit from my friend Tony B. Quick because second nap at 12:30 p.m. until about 3 p.m.*
>
> *Tried to stay up for a lovely dinner with Mom and my good friend Kathy. Didn't make it :-(Mom and Kathy went to dinner while I just slept on Kathy's sofa for another few hours before racing home to go to bed! :-) Don't you wish you could have this much fun in one day?*
>
> *It is just odd. No serious headaches, no horrible pains, just an inability to even keep my head up. But, I am sitting up now, on cup of coffee number 2, and happy that Mom and friends are here to take care of yours truly!*

energy? When my fatigue was the worst, I didn't feel like I had the energy to raise my head off my pillow. You may find that you cannot focus or are not thinking clearly. You may not want to do any of the things you normally do. You may feel sad or irritable or negative. All of these are potential clues that you are dealing with fatigue.

The challenge with fatigue is that there is not a test that can be done that proves that you have it or the level you have. So, you have to share how you are feeling with your care providers so that they can assist you in managing it.

> **Donna**
>
> *Good Evening All,*
>
> *I hope this find you well! This finds me tired! :-)*
>
> *Work has been keeping me very busy with meetings going from 6:30 a.m. or 7 a.m. on all day. So, when I get to 5 p.m. it is nap time. Today, I am napping on the couch in anticipation of seeing my sister, Jennifer. The caretaker from Portland is on her way! Yeah! Just wish I felt well enough to do fun things all weekend with her. But, the reality is the Mack Truck is creeping up, and we know what that means. A few days of sleeping are on the way.*

Additionally, there is no magic pill or treatment to get rid of fatigue. However, as your care providers understand the extent of your fatigue, they may be able to support you with changes to treatments and other recommendations.

COPING WITH FATIGUE

One of the antidotes to fatigue your doctors and care team will advise you is to keep active. Depending upon your

> **Donna**
>
> *Oh my! So thankful my sister is here.*
>
> *As the fish Nemo would say, I keep telling myself "just keep swimming, just keep swimming!"*

capacity, go for a walk, to the gym for a tailored workout, or to a yoga class. Of course, talk to your doctor about the type of activity he or she recommends. Know that many medical centers as well as support centers such as Cancer Support Community and Gilda's Club offer movement classes specifically designed for those going through cancer treatments. If you already attend a class, ask the instructor if he or she can show you a modified workout.

There are alternative treatment therapies that can also help with fatigue and other side effects. Specially certified therapists can provide treatments, such as acupuncture, healing touch, or reflexology to try to minimize the fatigue. Keep in mind that your "toolbox" of options to deal with fatigue and other issues may involve much more than rest and medication.

- Acupuncture: Helpful with pain, nausea, fatigue and neuropathy
- Healing Touch: Helpful with anxiety and pain
- Aromatherapy: Helpful with anxiety and nausea
- Massage Therapy: Helpful with anxiety and pain

- Reflexology and Guided Imagery can also be helpful for some patients and side effects.

Another thing you can do is to plan your day knowing that naps will be involved. Recognize when you have the most energy and prioritize what you need to accomplish for the day during those active times, scheduling naps around the activities. One of the most critical things to understand when dealing with fatigue is that you will just have to let some things go. So, your bed may not get made, the dishes may be left in the sink, dinner out may be cancelled at times. Fatigue is all consuming, and letting go of the items on your "to do" list will enable you to rest and recover as needed. If letting some of these things go really bothers you, now is the time to ask for support from family and friends.

> **Donna**
>
> *Let's talk about fatigue tonight!!*
>
> *So, I have led my life always overdoing - just a little. :-). Even in my twenties I would have what I called "crash and burn" weekends. Basically, having been very active for months in a row, I would crash and burn by literally sleeping the weekend away. So, I figured I knew all about fatigue.... was I ever wrong! And it is so tough to explain. Yes, I am very tired, but there is more than that. Sometimes, I can't even hold my head up; it just lolls to the side. I actually forgo coffee in the morning, and pretty much anything else, as it is too exhausting to contemplate even walking to the kitchen, let alone fixing it. It is not just being tired. It is having no energy, no interest in anything; it is knowing that my mind is not processing as it should. I don't even feel pain as the lack of energy is so overwhelming.*
>
> *When the doctor told me to just rest for two weeks as I was so fatigued, I struggled with that. As usual my body and mind are at war with my mind screaming get over it and just do. But, my body just can't. This being the second week, though, I see great improvement. I only sleep about an hour or two during the day and 10 hours or so at night (compared to 12 to 14 hours a night and four hours during the day last week).*
>
> *The good news is, this is feeling more like just being tired. That I can handle. This fatigue thing, it absolutely wore me out!!*

Another strategy, for when you are feeling your worst, is to place necessary items within easy reach. Really, you might ask? Yes. If it is exhausting to make a cup of tea, you won't do it. Of course, drinking your fluids will help to mitigate the fatigue. So,

> **Donna**
>
> *Just a little note to whine. :-). I am so exhausted and wish this constant pain from the incisions under my arms and into my back would stop. I bet then I could sleep through the night and get back to normal Donna shenanigans!*
>
> *There are a few new funny stories to tell, but they are on hold until I get my energy back up. In the meantime, you all keep smiling; I will just keep sleeping.*

anything you can do on the days you have some energy to make your fatigue days easier will be helpful. I kept tissue, hand lotion, and lip balm in virtually every room as the dryness I experienced really bothered me. I also filled the large hospital style water bottles with lots of ice and water and kept one right next to me, and the other in the refrigerator to be sure of drinking my water each day.

I learned the hard way that when I was feeling fatigued, I needed to give in to it. When I tried to shake it off and just keep going, I was even more exhausted the following day. Doing calming activities that you enjoy can also help you handle the fatigue. Reading was one of my favorite activities, and I lost myself in many novels during my journey. Others enjoy movies, music, or tapes specifically designed to encourage calm relaxation. Whatever is your calming pleasure, now is the time to use it.

Something that *sounds* like a good antidote to fatigue may not always turn out to be so, though. One friend wanting to do something fun, and perhaps therapeutic, suggested a spa day. I loved the idea. However, I was really quite fatigued at the time, and I didn't really think it through. I thought I would come away rejuvenated; I just was more tired and sore afterward. Getting a massage did not relieve but exacerbated the muscle aches that often accompanied my fatigue. The hot tub, which I so love, not only zapped me of the rest of my energy,

Donna

Hello Everyone....

Some pieces of good news to report tonight! 1. My heart is fine. 2. My lungs are fine. Oh, wait, you didn't realize I had concerns? Well, let me fill you in! ☺ So this breathing thing is still a problem. I had only received three water pills on Thursday. So, come Monday, my breathing was as bad as ever. Monday morning I did a Pulmonary Function Test. I finished that and called my oncologist, wondering what we should do. She called in a prescription for more of the water pill. I headed to radiation, huffing and puffing with every step. As I was leaving, the oncologist called. They wanted me to go immediately to the Cancer Institute to do an echo-cardiogram to see how my heart was working. Huffing and puffing I drove out to the Cancer Institute. The breathing was so bad that when I got into registration, I asked for a wheelchair, very uncharacteristically, may I add. So, I did the echo, and the cardiologist read it, staying late in case he might have to admit me. Well, the heart is fine. I was free to go home.

Fast forward to this morning, when I received a call from the infusion room. The doctor wanted to see me... again. So, I headed back out. Well, she said, your lung test was absolutely normal. Not a problem at all with O2, your breathing, etc., etc.

Your echo - absolutely fine. Your heart beats very strongly. There is a little fluid there, but nothing of significance. Given all the chemo, it is absolutely fine. So, why couldn't I breathe normally? That was the question. Additionally, why did the water pill help? They suspect that there was some fluid around my heart, so removing that is assisting my breathing. The challenge is...no matter what they consider as a possibility, my tests (CAT scan of lungs, pulmonary and echo) show everything to be normal. Paging Dr. House.... :-)?

One remote possibility is that the radiation is causing some fibrous growth around my heart, but again, they should have seen it on the echo or CAT scan. So, they gave me an inhaler and said that if I have the problems, to use that and see if it might help. It certainly won't hurt. And off I drove to the radiation oncologist. While I drove, the radiation oncologist and medical oncologist conferred. The RO doesn't believe it is the radiation. And, if it is, they would put me on steroids. Guess what steroids do? They cause you to retain water! So, we don't really want that...again.

The net of this: They think my body is just very fatigued from everything. So, I am to rest, rest, rest. No going out, no shopping, no more than four hours of work at most, no errands, no leg physical therapy. I have seven more treatments to go, and they want to just get me through the radiation with rest, the inhaler, and the water pills. But the good news is...a strong heart and good lungs! :-)

but I later learned that the heat could worsen the lymphedema in my arm.

I am not suggesting that you NOT go to a spa or do another equally relaxing activity you enjoy. What I am suggesting is that you really have to listen to your body and consider how the activity will impact you. I may still have gone to the spa, as I love the relaxing environment; however, the lap pool and a facial or pedicure would have been better options for me while I was fatigued.

COMPLICATIONS

Fatigue can lead to additional concerns. If you find yourself becoming confused or unable to focus your thoughts, make a call to your care provider. If you become short of breath or your heart races with just the littlest bit of activity, make a call to your care provider.

A significant issue that I experienced with my fatigue was ongoing shortness of breath. As I moved from chemo treatments to radiation, my fatigue and therefore shortness of breath became much worse. There was no easy cure for this. While the doctors tried to minimize the shortness of breath for me, resting was the most effective strategy.

These treatments tax your body to the limit, and the order of your treatments can also impact your fatigue levels. I later learned that when radiation follows chemo, the doctors are finding many people having a much more difficult time with radiation and, as a result, even more fatigue. Many of your body's functions from digestion to circulatory and everything in between are struggling with fatigue. A vicious cycle develops as you continue to get treatments: While you are already fatigued, you can't easily emerge from the cloud of fatigue.

As the fatigue deepens, other functions become impacted, such as I experienced with shortness of breath.

Keep a close watch on your fatigue. It may be a side effect you mention the most. Notice I say mention, as we ladies don't really complain, do we? While there are no magic treatments to resolve fatigue, you can mitigate it by staying active, resting when needed, and drinking your fluids.

Donna

Hello all....

Well, radiation ended with a whimper! As excited as I was to see this end, I was too tired to celebrate. I left radiation and came home to sleep - all day Thursday, most of Friday, and so far, a good bit of today. So much has gone on, and I have come such a long way. I have just been too tired to share everything. But, as my energy returns, I will slowly start filling in the pieces here.

First of all, those who have called and I haven't responded - I apologize. Breathing and sleeping have been my main priorities the past several weeks. Please know how much I cherish your calls and messages, even if I don't respond in a timely fashion!!

LIFE - CANCER BALANCE

A dear friend lost his mother recently to cancer. He tells me that his mother always felt there were two types of women with cancer: those who talk about it and those who don't. Now, this may get a chuckle out of you, but I was not very sure which camp I belonged in. Really, Donna, you are saying, you are writing a book on it. True. But, when I first learned of my diagnosis, I shared it only with my family and friends primarily through a private blog I wrote. I did not want anyone at work to know. So, in fact, I did have a foot in both ponds, at least for a while.

As I began working on this book, I learned that many people don't talk about the fact that they have or have had cancer. They don't share what they are experiencing, even with family members. Which leads to an interesting question: How do you balance everything, cancer, your family, your friends, your work, your treatments, your side effects, especially if you are not talking about it?

To begin with, there is no perfect answer. We are individuals with distinct needs and situations. But as much as we struggle for balance in our lives, when we find out we have cancer, that balance is thrown completely out of whack. Something that many women mention is that as they go through cancer treatment, it is often the first time that they have had to put themselves first. However, cancer has to take a priority over other parts of our lives, for if we don't tackle it, the consequences are dire.

To Tell Or Not To Tell

A basic, starting question for many ladies is whether they want to talk about their cancer or not. Are they comfortable sharing their story? When it comes to discussing your cancer, what is right for you? Start by thinking about how you naturally handle things. If you typically are willing to share quite a bit, that may feel automatic and appropriate to you. If you tend to be private, that will be a more comfortable space for you. Recognize that communicating about your cancer and your treatments will keep it front and center for you. Also, recognize that you will need to coach others on how to talk about your cancer with you: You will need to let them know if you are open to questions from them or would rather not discuss it at all, or are comfortable with some level of discussion in between.

Why do so many women keep a cancer diagnosis private? There are many reasons, a primary one being that women don't want to be defined by their cancer; they don't want the "stigma" of cancer associated with them, so they keep it quiet. In some cases, they don't want the cancer to be a burden on friends or family, so they don't share it. Others I talked to said that they had neglected taking care of themselves with regular doctor visits and were embarrassed that they now had cancer. One woman shared that she kept her diagnosis of lymphoma from her entire family as she didn't want the "drama" associated with them knowing of her illness. Another woman said that she kept it a secret so as not to upset her parents. This is *your* journey, and for that reason, communication about it should be whatever is comfortable for you.

If you want your diagnosis to be kept more private, you will need to let your family and friends know that so that they do not share beyond what is comfortable for you. If you are comfortable sharing, then again, letting your family and friends know that is important as well. My family comes from the keep it very private perspective, and I started off that way. However, as my journey progressed, I shared more and more, eventually even telling those I worked with about the diagnosis. In the end, I was very transparent about my journey, to a large extent because I was quickly discovering that the information I was learning was helpful to others.

As you consider your view of communicating your cancer, recognize that there may be different levels of communication for different groups; your family, friends, work associates, etc. Also, recognize that as you work through your treatments, you will become fatigued and various side effects may impact how you feel. Of course, as you struggle with treatments, well-meaning family and friends will want to talk with you even more to see how you are feeling, which can be, of course, exhausting. A friend introduced me to Caring Bridge, a wonderful website for keeping family (and friends if you desire) updated. I quickly started using it to share information as even before treatments

> **Donna**
>
> *Hello Everyone,*
>
> *Gosh, this is one tuckered out worker bee! I had a great day at this new job. The people are fabulous, which is so critical. The only hiccup was that my computer isn't working yet. But, I turned the lack of computer into a positive (at least for me) by leaving early so I could respond to e-mails. The key people there have been sending me e-mails to my home for a few weeks now, so I can easily work on things from home, where my computer works. Meanwhile, if I am lying down while I work, so I can rest, all the better - right :-)*
>
> *Overall, I faired pretty well. A bloody nose in the afternoon, common for me, but not too ladylike :-) when you are at a new job! Exhaustion is the big thing. I am going to have to get used to chemo without a nap in middle of the afternoon. By the way, speaking of being tired, guess who now has a business trip to Minneapolis on Wednesday and Thursday! You got it! We shall see how I fare. I think all I need to do is keep my wig on, bring lots of make-up, and never stop smiling!*

started, I became exhausted from simply talking about it hours on end. By the way, Caring Bridge can be set up so that only those you approve can see your blog, so it is a great vehicle to use to post updates when you don't want everyone to find you, a la Facebook.

WORK - CANCER BALANCE

I was a worker bee, always at the office. I do not have children, so my balance was very much between my work, my everyday life, and this new demon called cancer.

For my part, I interviewed for a major global head of marketing position at a Fortune 100 company on the day I learned I had cancer. Even going into the interview, I knew the type of news I might be hearing later that day regarding my biopsy. Yet, I needed to work, so I interviewed.

Once the diagnosis was confirmed, I talked to the oncologist about the immediate future: "Do I take this big job?" was the first question. After a long pause, she told me to take the job as she wanted *me* focused on living; she would focus on the cancer. Can I handle a job like this, while I go through treatment? "Yes," she explained; she could keep most of my symptoms at bay. "Can I travel?" I asked. Yes, that would not be a problem. "My boss lives in Brussels," I explained. "Can I travel internationally?" "Yikes, call me first," was her response.

So, my doctors felt confident I could do this, but what should I say to my employer and co-workers? Importantly, how would I balance this new job with the treatments required? I connected with a lawyer who worked on HR issues to advise me. I didn't want to say anything until I had accepted the job at the earliest, as I was fearful that if they knew I had cancer, they would pull the offer from me. But, at the same time, I usually prefer to be transparent, so not telling them didn't feel right. I also argued with myself that, fundamentally, I did not want to be known for having cancer. I wanted to be known for my abilities, my strength in brand building and leadership.

Initially, I did not tell the people at work that I had cancer and was undergoing treatments. I started my new job halfway through my chemo treatments, and by then I had a better understanding of my good and bad days. My big concern? Which wig should I to choose to wear to work? I knew once I showed up with one wig, I would need to wear it consistently or else people might wonder about my hair.

My not telling people at work, I later learned, is very common. Many, many people keep their cancer a secret at work. The issue consistently revolves around not letting cancer define you, being perceived as weak or less able. From an employment perspective, that fear leads to other fears, including could I be fired, laid-off, or let go? (While this is against the law, the personal fears are still there.) Might I not be promotable anymore? Might I be excluded from meetings and travel as teammates try to "protect" me? Very real fears for those working while going through cancer.

I was eventually forced into sharing that something was wrong when I was raced to the hospital and had to miss work for a few days. Fortunately, I was about eight weeks into the position and had been able to demonstrate my competency in the job. So, the reaction from the office was one of concern and support, which was so outstanding. I never did explain that I had already gone through most of my chemo. They just knew that cancer had been found and that I would need surgery and probably radiation.

Family - Cancer Balance

Being a mom, managing your family and going through cancer is a very difficult balancing act. As easy as it is to say, take care of yourself and your cancer first, the women I spoke with

> **Ellen**
> *I focused on my life, not myself. My life includes my children, my husband, my work, my friends. That focus gave me strength.*

expressed how inordinately difficult this was. Women by their very nature are nurturing and caretakers of others, so taking care of themselves is difficult for many.

Children need their mothers, and mothers will not let their children down. Several moms explained that by focusing on their children, they found the strength to deal with the challenges of cancer treatment. A common refrain was that focusing on children kept their attention off their disease, while inspiring them to do what needed to be done to take care of the disease and be there for their children.

> **Ellen**
> *My children so wanted to help me, to add value to this cancer journey, to do **something**. In a sewing class my 15 year old daughter decided she would make me cancer caps. She ended up making quite a few in different colors and designs. Some fun and silly, some simply elegant. They were wonderful. Yes, they were comfortable. More importantly, as I wore them, they were a constant reminder to both of us what she was doing to help me in this journey.*

One of the first things that many women mentioned to me is the simple energy of children. As you are fatigued, your children seem to have the energy that never stops. Calling on friends and family to take the children out, have play dates, cart them around to various activities became critical for moms trying to balance their life and cancer.

Another common issue is determining how to discuss your cancer with your children, or if you even should. Most women offered that they did not discuss the cancer with their very young ones. However, as a child got to the age of eight and nine or so, they could tell that there was something going on with mom that was more than just the flu, and transparency was actually helpful to the child. At this age, the children could actually provide some support for the mom if she was fatigued, by doing simple jobs around the house.

Moms often shared with me that cancer was turned into an opportunity for a family to come together, to become more tightknit, to battle the disease as a team. The children want to help their mother through the illness and at the same time feel so helpless. What can they do? One father sat his children down and explained that as a family team working through this illness, the children were going to have to do more around the house, help with laundry, help with the cleaning, and that importantly, they needed to do what was asked with a smile and no complaining.

While it is one thing to tell the children that a parent has cancer, it is an entirely different thing to help the children talk through their fears and concerns. There are a variety of programs that provide support to families and especially children to address the fear and concerns they have when a parent has cancer. Cancer Support Communities and Gilda's Clubs are among the organizations offering such programs.

CHEMO - LIFE BALANCE

Balancing your everyday life when going through chemo can be a challenge. A common concern is fatigue and how limiting that can be. Whether you are managing a family, running to an office, or leading your busy life, you may not have the luxury of a nap every afternoon. From a work perspective, if you can coordinate with your supervisor and potentially work from home, or arrange for flexible hours, that may be helpful when exhaustion hits and a nap is needed.

For the moms with demanding schedules, those I interviewed indicated that having support from friends in taking children to after school activities was critical as they managed their fatigue. Another woman commented she was just too fatigued to make meals, and that friends had arranged to have dinners delivered to the house every day. They had a cooler on the front porch, and friends would leave the dinner for the family in the cooler. One great advantage of this approach was that while she was resting, dinner was being delivered.

Keep in mind that not only is the fatigue a potential issue as you balance your life, but also missed time for treatments and appointments. I knew my chemo was a five to seven hour day experience. Therefore, on my chemo day I would not be able to go to the office at all. Again, because working remotely was a possibility for me, I took advantage of that

> **Donna**
>
> *Hello Everyone,*
>
> *I can't explain adequately this sheer exhaustion that I have. At least I understand it better. Yesterday I left the office at 3:15 p.m. headed home to take a nap, and then did a bit more work. Today I barely made it to noon before I left for home. What is concerning is that I am so tired, my eyes heavy as I drove home both days.*
>
> *Today, when I got home I laid down on the sofa with my laptop on me and spent the afternoon on conference calls. But I just don't feel right leaving early in the day. I want to be at the office; I should be there meeting people. But, I can hardly function. At least today at home I was able to take 15 minute cat naps twice between phone calls. I keep telling myself that as long as I am performing, we are ok. They certainly seem very pleased, and I am getting everything done, but still.... shouldn't I be there in person?*
>
> *Well, time for another nap! I have a conference call with our Asia marketing team tonight at 8 p.m., so I better rest up.*
>
> *Sweet dreams all...*

and worked as I received chemo. I did coordinate with the oncology nurses and team in advance, and they would make sure I was in a secluded area of the infusion room. I would set up my laptop, plug in my phone, and I was off and running, taking phone calls and meetings remotely from chemo. If you would like to work through your chemo, do make sure that you connect with your chemo team first. They are trying to keep all the patients comfortable, and noisy phone calls are often not acceptable.

Chemo days are a good time to enlist the support of family and friends interested in helping you. They can take you to your appointments, take care of the children, run any errands for that day, or simply be with you through this treatment. Keep in mind that typically infusion rooms will limit the number of visitors to one, two at the most. Simply there is not a lot of room for multiple chairs near you and the nurses need free access to your IVs and port. Secondly, usually a number of patients are receiving chemo in the same room. Chemo affects everyone differently, so having a number of guests may be disturbing to other patients who are not feeling well or trying to sleep. Also, it is not recommended that children go into infusion rooms. Not only can seeing such sick people be overwhelming for the little ones, but in addition, children are notorious for carrying lots of germs, something any chemo patient needs to avoid.

Be prepared for the fact that as you go through chemo, you will typically have "bad" days following your infusion. You will figure out when *your* bad days are usually after your first chemo. I expected it to be around day two or three, but learned that about five days after I received chemo is when I really felt horrible, that my infamous Mack truck hit. On those days, the fatigue, body aches, and headaches would be the worst for me, and I had a hard time functioning.

Knowing this, I tried to schedule my chemo so that my bad days would fall over the weekend. That way, I was not missing work when I was feeling my worst. My chemo cycles were three weeks long, which meant the first week I received the chemo and then felt the worst four or five days later. The second and third week were recovery weeks, so to speak, and then the cycle began again.

Your chemo type, delivery method, and schedule will be unique. Working up front with your doctor to understand your chemo schedule and what to expect can help you determine when you need the most help and how to balance this treatment with the other parts of your life.

SURGERY - LIFE BALANCE

Surgery - life balance is very different for every patient and can be very intense. Your needs and expectations may be different depending on the type and severity of the surgery. Recovery can be anywhere from several days to several weeks. If you have major surgery, expect to rest for four to eight weeks. Of course, that is highly dependent on your risk factors and how you are recovering.

Two immediate considerations as you recuperate are range of

> **Donna**
>
> *Guess who's going back to work on Monday? Ok, so it is part-time. But, then the following Monday the doctors think I can go back full time (4 weeks or so from my last surgery).*
>
> *The doctor couldn't have been more pleased with everything. Yes, I am in pain; I will save that story for another time.*
>
> *For now, let's celebrate. A little work on the horizon, and I was at a great party last night with some dear friends and met some lovely new friends. (A sip, sup and swap party - sip some wine, have a bite to eat, and swap books with each other! A great idea!) Hmmmm... could it be that Donna is getting back to some of her old shenanigans!!*
>
> *Three cheers for bodies that heal, as my vet brother-in-law has frequently reminded me. We are blessed in that way....*

motion and pain management. As long as you are on significant pain medications, often causing grogginess, you will be limited in your ability to drive and to focus. Your doctors will gradually move you to something like Tylenol for pain management, which, if successful, will allow you to resume more of your everyday life.

Range of motion limitations may last for a while, depending on the surgery you have had. For instance, if you have had a mastectomy or double mastectomy, being able to get your arms back over your head may be several weeks or more away. Something as simple as removing dishes from a cabinet may not be allowed for the first six weeks post surgery and too painful the following several weeks or months.

In order to prepare for living through this phase of your treatment, be sure to discuss with your care team your return to normal activities in great detail before you have the surgery. What type of support might you need when you return home? When will you be allowed to drive? When may you return to work? What are limitations in movement or lifting items?

> **Donna**
>
> *Sometimes I just want to scream from the rooftops... "I DON'T HAVE THE ENERGY TO MAKE YOU HAPPY...."*
>
> *Ok, I didn't scream it, but I typed it in caps. Maybe it's out of my system. You see, when my day starts at 7 a.m. with calls from work, with everyone wanting something, and I am still struggling to find the energy to eat a banana every morning (as Mom suggests), we have a problem.*
>
> *And everyone, and I mean EVERYONE at work, says just rest and take care of yourself. But then the calls come. "I just have one little question for you – it's really easy." How do I tell them that nothing in my life is easy right now? And everyone just has one little question....*
>
> *Ok - my complaints are out of my system now. For those also going through this, now you know: sometimes little miss sunshine here can't exactly smile either. ☺*
>
> *The truth is out....*
>
> *But, I am headed to dinner with Patty and Deborah. If anyone can get me laughing, it is these two. And then after dinner, I will remind myself that a weekend of rest is only two days away!*
>
> *Love to all...*

I discovered that I would not be able to use my arms much for several weeks. In fact, for the first several weeks, I could not even use them to get myself in and out of bed. Fortunately, my surgeon advised me of this. A friend suggested that I rent a recliner to use as my bed. This ended up being the best investment ever. I called Rent-a-Center, and they dropped one off that worked by using my legs and feet to lean the chair back or pull it forward, which worked out perfectly. If a double mastectomy is in your future, this tip is critical. It will save your arms, chest, and shoulders from so much pain.

It is amazing how quickly the doctors get you up, moving, and returning home post surgery. Even with a double mastectomy, I returned home the next day. While you may be home, you will need help. Between your pain management, limited movement, fatigue and potential nausea, having people available to assist with your recovery is key. Realize that depending on the nature of your surgery and level of pain, you may spend the next several days simply sleeping.

> **Donna**
>
> *Now another thing people need to know is that when you have a mastectomy, it is very common to get shoulder impingements or rotator cuff injuries. Yet another thing I would have loved to have known in advance!*
>
> *The cancer side is working really well! The non-cancer side, on the other hand, is now giving me problems as my shoulder locks as I try to raise my hand over my head.*

Expect to be given some post surgery activities to help get you back to your normal life sooner rather than later. I had breathing exercises to do several times a day. I also began occupational and physical therapy fairly quickly after surgery. The goal of the occupational therapy was to reduce scar tissue as well as limit the possibility of lymphedema. The physical therapy was designed for my right shoulder. During a double mastectomy, it is common that the arm, on the opposite side of the cancer, be positioned at a 90 degree angle for several hours.

Shoulder pain and issues, such as impingement, can result, as I experienced, and physical therapy can help to manage the pain and encourage normal movement.

The piece to recognize is that as you are healing and trying to find that life-surgery balance, your recovery might include multiple therapy appointments a week, something I had not counted on. Such therapy and other follow-up appointments coupled with continued fatigue, pain, and limited mobility will likely be your reality for the first several weeks post surgery.

RADIATION - LIFE BALANCE

Radiation treatments most typically occur after surgery and are designed to destroy any remaining cancer cells in the area. Often they occur everyday for a series of weeks and do not last long, perhaps 30 minutes, more or less. Of course, as with everything, it depends: on your cancer, your body, your treatment approach. (See the chapter Burn, Burn, Burn for more information on radiation.)

Your first several treatments may take a little longer as you first get set on the machine, and they make sure placement is correct. However, as treatment continues, you and your radiation team become very comfortable with the approach and requirement, and the session can move rather quickly.

> **Donna**
>
> *Work was a zoo today. So, I am sitting at the hospital waiting for more tests, when my boss calls all freaked out. Apparently someone suggested we hadn't gotten something done in time for the big launch next week. So, in between my gasps for air, I was dialing everyone asking what happened.*
>
> *Turns out everything was fine. She just jumped, assuming the worst, and caused everyone to panic. Anyhow, I solved that. Work associates kept saying I shouldn't be on the phone, but I was the one calm voice today. Other things seem more critical to me.*

I chose to have my treatments in the afternoon at the same time every day. I was fairly productive in the mornings, but by afternoons, was quite fatigued. So, getting things done in the morning, going to radiation, and then calling it a day worked for me. I did work all the way through my radiation. Since my office was aware of my cancer by this time, we were able to schedule meetings around radiation, and if a conversation was required post radiation, I could do that from home lying down.

My radiation lasted for four weeks. The first two weeks I handled it fairly well. However, come the third week, the fatigue started to take its toll. A serious side effect I experienced was shortness of breath. It was hard to determine specifically what was causing this, but, some combination of the chemo, all the surgeries, and the radiation caused some significant issues and additional hospital visits.

Until the breathing issues were under control, my activities were limited. I often had to lie down as it was much worse just

> **Donna**
>
> *Phew, what a day!!!*
>
> *I was supposed to be on a flight right now to NJ.... But...the doctors stepped in and said no way!*
>
> *So, here is the deal. I was on the phone with the main three doctors' offices today- oncologist, breast surgeon, plastic surgeon - as we discussed single vs. double mastectomy. Well, my voice was a little gravelly, and so they all asked about that. While I haven't felt sick, there is no denying that I have been exhausted this weekend. Then they asked if my ankles were swollen. My ankle is almost always swollen, so the answer was yes. Next thing you know I was hearing that I was absolutely not to travel. And, oh, by the way, please swing over to the Mercy Cancer and Breast Institute for blood work and a chest x-ray.*
>
> *The problem being, if I am coming down with anything, they need to get me on and off antibiotics before surgery. So, I head back to the oncologist tomorrow to see whether I am coming down with something or not. Meanwhile, I was jumping around canceling my flights and changing all my meetings for the next several days. Work, by the way, was great saying I should do what the doctors ask and not worry about it.*
>
> *Anyhow, what a crazy day!*

sitting up. I had people drive me to appointments as it seemed very dangerous for me to be on the road. Therapy appointments were cancelled, and naturally work was severely limited.

TRAVEL

Whether you travel for work or for fun, your travel may be impacted as a result of your treatments. Be exceptionally careful with air travel. Not only is it tiring for an already fatigued body, but the air can be rich with viruses and bacteria. Taking products such as AirBorne may minimize your risk of infection. Another tip I learned was to put a little Aquaphor on a Q-tip and apply it to the entrance of my nose. The Aquaphor can serve as a barrier, preventing bacteria from getting up and in. Of course, if you are dealing with shortness of breath or other lung issues, that approach may not be recommended.

In the end, I did take several short trips in the U.S. while I was on chemo, and while I hated to do so, asked for a wheel chair on occasion. I learned to try to "save" my energy for when I really needed it. If I traveled in the morning, knowing I had meetings in the afternoon, I would not waste my energy walking the airport.

What I started to learn was that there is sequencing and timing to the treatments. Surgery had to be done within a few weeks of the chemo, or, another round or two of chemo would be required for me. The possibility of getting sick from a flight was very high due to my fatigue. The potential consequence of delaying surgery and then additional rounds of chemo if I did get sick were completely unacceptable, so, I cancelled the travel. The advice my doctor gave me in the very beginning was so critical: Call if you are travelling.

Car trips are a little bit different in that you are not sitting in an enclosed environment with strangers who may be carrying various illnesses. However, a car trip can be exhausting, especially when dealing

> **Donna**
>
> *Good Evening All,*
>
> *One of the challenges of chemo is, of course, a compromised immune system. Many people whom I've talked to who have battled through this talk about not going out: staying home, not going to restaurants, stores, or into crowds in order to avoid picking up anything.*
>
> *Of course, what do I do? Start a new job with lots of people and try to live my normal "out and about" life as usual. So, what to do.... stay inside and play it safe OR live life as best I can and deal with the occasional "cold" consequence?*

with fatigue. Since most of my family is in the midwest, we usually travel by car to see each other. It was many months post all my treatments before I felt I had the energy to drive myself to see them. In the meantime, people traveled to me, or I would catch rides with others traveling in that general direction.

I wish there was some magic answer for how to achieve cancer-life balance for you. The best I can advise is that you have to put yourself and your treatments first. How active you want to be or can be otherwise will vary at different stages of your illness and treatment. Importantly, your treatments need to go on as scheduled, as prescribed, and then you can pay attention to the other parts of your life. So very difficult, I understand, whether you are a mom, a wife, a sister, a boss, a daughter, a lady.

FABULOUS FUTURE

LIVING RADIANTLY POST CANCER

Donna

Just a brief check-in...

You know everything seems a bit surreal right now: one day you have cancer; the next day you just get on with your life.

And so I have...doing way too much each day, which goes without saying! What is odd is that I keep thinking I am forgetting something - like a doctor's appointment. But I don't have any scheduled for a bit.

So the question I ponder now is what is "normal" life now, post cancer? Will it change? Will it be the same as my life used to be? What will I have learned? Time will tell, I think. I will let you know....

I kept hearing from friends, cancer survivors, and the medical community about my "new normal" post cancer, but I really didn't understand what that was. In my world, there always had been normal and not normal, so I had to figure out how to process the idea of a "new normal."

To an extent, I started to understand what people were trying to say as soon as I was finished with all of my treatments. For about 11 months, everything about my life had been scheduled around my various treatments. Work meetings always took a back seat to radiation treatments. Whether I got together with a friend was dependent on how I was handling my fatigue. My family visited based on my chemo and surgery schedules. Then, one day, that stopped. The oncologist said, "I will see you in three months." Wow! Now what?

Return Of Energy

In typical Donna form, when I heard I was finished with treatments and didn't need to see the doctor for three months, I thought I was fine. That "boom," my energy would be back and my life would go back to what it had always been. I was wrong. When I complained that it was taking so long for my energy to return, the doctors explained that I should count on feeling like my "old" self about a year after my last treatment (for me, radiation). Really, I couldn't believe that. Yet, as I think about all the things my body had to handle to get me past the cancer, it made sense. This journey is tough on your spirit, on your physical body, on you; it will take awhile to recuperate.

Even now three plus years after I finished treatment, I am still much more cognizant of my energy levels. If I am feeling exhausted, I rest. That is something I would never have done pre-cancer. I was the push through and don't let anything stop you type of gal. I learned to listen to my body, know when it feels fatigued, and be willing to cancel or delay things to give my body the rest it needs.

When I don't listen to my body telling me it is fatigued, I become short of breath, a side effect I may always live with because of some damage my lungs suffered during treatments. When it happens, I have no choice but to sit down and rest.

I didn't expect that a side effect could linger for even years later. But, it can and does happen. The difference is, once you are past your treatments, you understand the effect and why it might be happening and then, importantly, what to do to resolve it.

Things To Know

Once you have had cancer and certain treatments, there are things you might not be able to do. I did not realize all the precautions that would be needed, for the rest of my life, down the road.

For the breast cancer patient, if lymph nodes were removed in your arm, you should never have your blood pressure taken on that side again. The removal of lymph nodes can cause lymphedema to occur, and anything tight around your arm can trigger the lymphedema. So, you will have to tell your caregivers, each time you see them. The nurse may naturally grab the closest arm, which could be the one that was impacted, and it will be up to you to tell him or her no, use the other side.

Speaking of lymphedema, if you suffered with that at all, you may need to get a compression sleeve and a gauntlet for your hand to be used off and on through the course of your life. For instance, their use is commonly recommended for air travel to prevent swelling. This is especially true for long flights. The recommendation is to put the sleeve on about two hours before you leave the ground and keep it on about two hours after you land, so that you arm can get re-accustomed to the air pressure on land. Be prepared, though. In my experience, many TSA screeners in the U.S. are not familiar with compression sleeves, and I often have additional screening as a result.

Another interesting post cancer issue is that I am not able to use heat post surgery, anywhere near the cancer site, such as to treat my sore shoulder. Because heat speeds up metabolic processes, and cancer is metabolic in nature, there is concern that if there are any cancer cells remaining that any heat treatments on the cancer side of my upper body could stimulate the cancer's growth. Even all these months later, ice is the go to option to treat muscle soreness on the upper left side of my body.

TREATMENT EFFECTS

Your treatments may have some lasting effects as well that you want to be aware of. With chemo, of course, comes hair loss, dry skin, change in taste sensation, fatigue, etc., etc. In the last chapter of this book I talk about the fact that your hair will come back. But, let's address some of these others issues here. My skin had been dry pre-cancer, super-duper dry during cancer, and back to just plain dry post cancer. It takes a long time for the moisture to be replenished in your skin. Some people mention dealing with dry skin after chemo for as long as a year or more, so don't be surprised if that is the case for you, as your skin takes a beating after all. Your sense of taste will most likely go back to normal, although it can still take a few months post treatment before things taste as good as you remember. The fatigue can take minimally a full year after your final treatment before you really feel like it is gone. Even then, I found myself exhausted three years post treatment and discovered that not only can it pop back up a few years later, but that post treatment medications can cause fatigue as well.

Chemo treatments also pose a risk of developing osteopenia, a precursor to osteoporosis. Remember that your bones are greatly impacted by your chemo treatments, so this is one to look out for post treatment. With proper treatment, osteopenia can be reversed. Osteoporosis, once developed, usually cannot be reversed. A simple bone scan can help to determine if this is something you need to be concerned with or not.

Another common post cancer problem is neuropathy, damage to the nerves, those that impact your senses, your mobility, or your automatic nervous system (things that happen that you do not control, such as sweating). Neuropathy can occur from a variety of factors from the chemo, itself, to surgery to medications and may be felt as a tingling or burning sensation, depending on the nerves impacted. While it typically cannot be reversed, the doctors can work with you to manage the pain or discomfort you feel.

Aside from neuropathy, the surgical implications for you post cancer tend to revolve around mobility. In the course of having surgery, many things may have been cut from muscle, skin, and lymph systems to other larger organs. As these heal, you may experience limitations, often the result of scar tissue, which can be very tight and fibrous, that forms at the site of the incision. An important part of your recovery from surgery may be occupational and/ or physical therapy. If prescribed for you, do those therapies! So many times I have heard of people who decided to wait, or not do them, for whatever reason. However, these therapies are designed to improve your range of motion, and that includes breaking down scar tissue that may be forming. You may even have to be the one to suggest to your doctor a therapy evaluation. If you find your are limited in movement or have pain as you move, and a therapy has not been prescribed yet, ask whether an evaluation by a therapist might be beneficial. If advised, he or she will provide exercises or other modalities of treatment that can increase range of motion, manage pain, or break-up the scar tissue created.

Concerns And Fears

Once you have had cancer, that fear, that concern, may always be there. Over time, you may be able to put it way into the back of your mind; however, it doesn't take much for it to come roaring back again. There are things that may trigger these concerns, so being on the lookout for them may help you manage the fears better.

Is It Just A Cold?

Quite simply, even the slightest cold may cause you to fear that cancer is returning. This is especially true as you first finish your treatments. But, even as the years go on, if a particular medical condition strikes, your first inclination may be to think that the cancer is back. As much as possible, be rational about your concern. The fear can be paralyzing. Don't let the fear control you or the situation. If the medical condition is new and different, a quick call to your doctor can help determine whether a test is required to check and see.

New Tests

Expect to have blood work regularly post cancer treatment. When you have first finished treatment, you may have blood work every three months or so for a year or two. As you continue to flourish, your follow-up visits and blood tests may move to every six months and, ultimately, every year or so.

While blood tests continue, new tests may occur, based on the cancer you had, the likelihood of recurrence, or the potential for metastases. These new tests can be really traumatic; I know they are for me. My type of cancer can metastasize to the brain. Therefore, at the three year past diagnosis point, I began to get annual brain scans. Even the thought that you are purposely going in to check for early cancers in another part of your body opens the floodgates of memories and fears of your cancer.

For many women that I spoke with, after having breast cancer, the fear associated with mammograms can be overwhelming. In fact, many women said that they chose to have the double mastectomy in large part due to the fear of another breast cancer. For those like me who have had a double mastectomy, there are no more mammograms ever, an odd situation as we as women expect to have mammograms every year. Instead, I have brain scans.

The point here is that your body will now be monitored and scanned as a result of the cancer you had. That management of your body may very well be different from your pre-cancer days, and that alone is enough to trigger fear and concern for you.

I mentioned earlier to try to be rational in your view of these situations. The practice of medicine is very pragmatic, scientific. Based on a situation, a series of actions occur that in all likelihood can provide the insight for a next series of actions. However, those actions may show up as a brain scan, a colonoscopy, additional mammograms, or something else altogether. And for you, that is personal. Recognize that the testing is to determine whether the cancer has hit again, and don't let the test, itself, paralyze you.

New Medications

After you have finished all your treatments, you can expect to be on a medication or two for a while. Many women post breast cancer are prescribed Tamoxifen for five years or so, as it is a drug that can limit estrogen production, which can be a key driver of breast cancer. For post-menopause women, an aromatase inhibitor might be recommended as it can limit production of estrogen. Tamoxifen is rather well known for side effects, such as hot flashes, but it is also well known for its great ability to reduce the risk of a cancer recurrence.

The challenge with many of the drugs used post cancer to reduce the risk of a recurrence is the side effects. In many cases there may be an alternative that may have a similar cancer negating effect should the side effects of a particular drug be intolerable. Of course, work with your doctor to understand your side effects, the best course of action to manage them, and whether an alternative medication may be appropriate.

All too often, women stop using a medication post cancer treatment because of the side effects. Of course, it doesn't help that every morning when you pop the pill, you are reminded that you had cancer. However, stopping a medication due to side effects is not wise, but that probably goes without saying.

LIVING RADIANTLY

Even as I re-read this chapter I think to myself, holy cow, there is a lot to consider even after the cancer is over. But, even with all of the things that can, might, do happen, we can live radiantly post cancer. And, by the way, I believe we can return to normal, not create a new normal.

I know in saying this that I am totally going against the grain, but here is the deal. To me, a new normal implies that my life will be forever changed, that I have to accept limitations in my life because of my cancer. I don't subscribe to that. I fully live my life, much as I did pre-cancer. Do I sometimes have a sense of dread when going in for a brain scan? Yes. But, I keep that fleeting. I don't dwell on it. Are there physical things I must do or that I now can't do? Aside from wearing a sleeve when I travel or having my blood pressure checked on the opposite side, no. Did I change my life because of the cancer? Well, I don't work the way I used to, but that is a good thing. And, I am eating better and working out more. So, yes, I changed, but perhaps that should have been my normal pre-cancer.

There is an important program, the STAR program, for Survivorship, Training and Rehab, which is designed to provide tools and support for cancer patients as they *regain* their normal life. This program certifies care providers in an effort to encourage cancer programs to work not only with the sick patient, but the surviving patient to return to her pre-cancer standard of living. As you move into your post-cancer phase, ask whether your hospital system is STAR certified. If it is, it can offer a variety of tools to support your wellness. The STAR program believes that you should not settle for a "new normal" if you want to return to your life and energy levels pre-cancer; they help you achieve that.

I have known people to create new normals when the fear of the cancer paralyzes them. I would offer you that cancer doesn't deserve the ability to totally change what is normal for you. The practice of medicine will manage the cancer. You can live radiantly and with the spirit you have always had. Are there some changes that will occur? Well, sure - different medical tests and the like. But, who you are, your radiant self, your ability to be, to influence, to make a difference to people, to live fully: Cancer cannot take that from you. Don't let it try.

IT ALL COMES BACK TO HAIR

It Will Grow Back

The good thing about hair is that it will grow back. Now, how long it takes is an entirely different matter. I finished my chemo in December and by the end of January, I saw a hair or two on my head!

Unfortunately, it took months before I had a full head of hair and could begin to shape it into a style. So, I stayed with my wigs for several months, post chemo.

When my hair began to grow back in, of course, I became anxious to speed up

> **Donna**
> *How long does your hair have to be before you begin washing it again? See, I have exactly five hairs hitting the two-inch long mark on top of my head. Mind you, the hair on the rest of my head has hardly "sprouted". ☺ My decision was pretty simple in the end. The arms hurt too much to get them above my head. Therefore, I concluded that five two-inch pieces of hair do NOT need to be washed!*

the process. The questions became, why was it taking months? I kept asking people, was there anything I could do? One of my therapists recommended I create a sea salt scrub and rub it on my head to remove dead skin cells while invigorating the hair to grow. The theory sounded good to me. I tried it a few times, and whether or not it helped, minimally, it felt good. Importantly, it afforded me an element of control again. Taking action when so much has been out of your hands is therapy in and of itself. Then, again, perhaps it did work, because about two weeks later, I got to wash my hair for the first time in months.

You may have heard that when your hair comes back, it comes back differently. Was that ever true with me! I always had long, thin, very fine blond hair. In fact, someone once told me I didn't have hair but

> **Donna**
>
> *I realize that there has been a burning question for all of you. So, let me provide the answer forthwith. On an 85 degree day in St. Louis, what happens to the wig when you put the top down on the convertible and go whipping down the highway? I am pleased to announce - the wig stays on!*
>
> *Happy St. Pat's Day. Here is hoping your day was as beautiful!*

feathers, and truly it was always flying away. However, after chemo, my hair came back in coarse, in very tight curls, and in a color I could not describe – a mixture of black and gray and red and white. So, as soon as I was able, I dyed the hair to at least get it down to one or two colors.

I wanted to dye my hair right back to blond. However, I learned that to take hair to blond, you actually bleach color out. With all those colors going on, which color was to be removed? So the better option was dying my hair or covering the color I had, so that at least it had more of one solid color. I chose red. I mean, why not? Never in my life had I been a redhead, so I thought I might as well take the opportunity to try it out. I will suggest that you confirm with your oncologist that you can color your hair. I did, and while she did not

have any concerns, other women were advised to wait a bit, depending on their situation.

My hair also grew back very unevenly. So, I would have

> **Donna**
>
> *My hair is growing back in. There is so much I don't understand....like why do I get blond fur on my face? What color exactly is this hair on my head? My eyebrows are back, and if they look dark to you, it is because I have them dyed already. They are coming in blond (which is normal). Now, I have a little spiky action going on atop my head, but what in the world? I can't even do a mohawk correctly; it is horizontal on me! Yikes! If I am brave, perhaps I can start wearing this hair out. It could be my "artsy" look!*

longish sections on one part of my head and virtually no hair on another part. Going to the salon to get what I did have cut and trimmed was so difficult! After not having any hair, the idea of cutting or trimming the strands I now had was very hard. However, it was so uneven, that the only chance of getting away from wearing a wig all the time was to start to shape it into something or another. The first hair cut was more of a trim to bring in a little shape and get all the hair more even. The result? A tight crop.

The very tight curls lasted for almost a year before my hair started to relax. However, to this day, three years later, it still has far more body than ever before. Women have different hair outcomes post chemo. Some retain tight curls and a different texture, others go back to their original hair type, and still others end up somewhere in the middle. The rule of thumb I heard was that after about three years, you will know what your hair will be like, and it most likely will stay that way a while.

Timing is a critical question when we consider the whole growing your hair back issue. I

> **Donna**
>
> *Life as a redhead...*
>
> *Truth be told...I had my hair highlighted LAST weekend! I had to get used to it before I talked about it. What I like best is that it doesn't look like "sick" hair anymore. It looks like it is meant to be this way.*
>
> *They couldn't take me to completely blond from the gray/black/white stuff I was getting post chemo. So, we went red first. Blond highlights may appear next.*
>
> *We shall see....*
>
> *Here is to having short hair on a hot day!!* ☺

completed chemo in December, washed my hair for the first time in early April, and got the first color and trim in July. I got back to my more normal length and the blond color I love about 12 to 14 months after all of that. So, it was really about 18 months total before I returned to my more normal look and style.

HAIR ON YOUR BODY

So while it seemed like it was taking forever for the hair on my head to grow back, some of the other hair came back rather quickly, although there is some hair that has never come back at all. The hair under my arms grew back in quickly; after several months of growth, though, it all but stopped. So, to this day, I rarely, if ever, need to shave.

I still don't have hair on my arms and have exactly five hairs on my left leg. I count them regularly, as it is just so odd! In interviewing for the book, many women told me that they, too, are left with no hair in certain places or just a little hair. Yes, the hair "down there" does grow back for some, though many women report that it grew back much thinner.

HAIR ON YOUR FACE

Now, your face, on the other hand, presents some rather peculiar situations. First of all, your nose hair typically grows back, thank heavens. Your eyebrows and

> **Donna**
> THE UGLY: So, while I was in Indiana I said to my sister Karen, it seems like I have hair on my face – it's blond - but I don't remember all of this. She said we all have hair on our face. I don't know; I felt like I was competing with my cats for most furry!

eyelashes also grow back, although my eyelashes had no sooner grown in than they all fell out again. I learned that it is common to have this residual effect post chemo. Since I was not taking any treatment when they fell out the second time, Latisse was prescribed and they quickly grew back.

The hair issue I found most unnerving is that my face grew hair, and lots of it! I learned that this is very common. As your hair grows back, often it grows back significantly on your face. It grows in close to your more normal hair color, and so can be a particular issue for those with dark hair.

I was fortunate in that mine came in blond. So, while there was a lot of fur, it was not always noticeable. Once I learned it was common, I also learned that facialists can remove it with derma planing, a procedure I had done about once a month for about six months that removed the dry skin and the hair. Then the growth really slowed down, and I didn't have to fight the furry face look.

Being Radiant

If ever there is a reason for this book, it is simply this: You should know as much as possible about what you can expect, even things like that hair on your face grows back quickly even as that on your head comes in slowly. These are some of the very issues that were driving me bananas as I went through my cancer journey. I could keep a smile on my face, and then all of a sudden experience something like fur on my face and wonder and worry why it was happening. I know I don't answer all the whys in this book; sometimes we just don't know why. I know I don't discuss all the things that might happen - you are unique - yet, I hope that you have picked up one or two things that make your journey a little easier and that maybe you will pass on to others.

I started this book with a chapter on losing your hair, so dramatic for many women as a first and very noticeable sign of their illness. I leave you with the realization that your hair will grow back, perhaps not as fast as you would like, perhaps not the way you want it to look, but, it will grow back. In between, there are so many things that will go on with your body. But, you can handle them, and you can handle them like the lady you are. I am not saying that it will be easy. But, I am saying that with a little knowledge, you can live radiantly, you can live like a lady. I wish each of you only the best as you continue on your journey.

DONNA'S TIMELINE

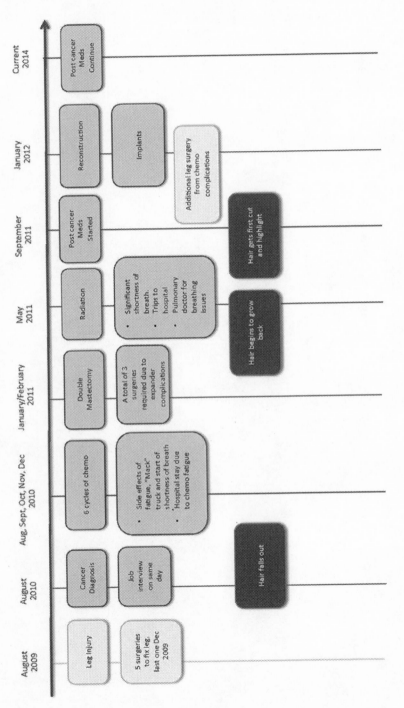

CONTRIBUTORS

So many radiant, wonderful people have made this book possible. They read and re-read sections, were interviewed, offered insights, suggestions, and prayers. My role was to coalesce the information while interspersing my story. Their knowledge and wisdom are what make this book so valuable and hopefully your journey through cancer as manageable and, in fact, radiant as possible. The credit truly goes to the following individuals without whose generous help this project could not have come to fruition.

Dr. Greg Camfield, Dentist

Lisa Chestnut, Lymphedema Specialist, Occupational Therapist

Dr. Maggi Coplin, Medical Oncologist

Johanna Crowe, Christian Dior Make-up and Skin Specialist for Saks Fifth Avenue

Elizabeth Ann Good, Spiritual Advisor

Dr. Judith Gurley, Plastic Surgeon

Matt Hopfer, Personal Trainer

Dr. Diane Radford, Surgical Oncologist

Dr. Michelle Smith, Integrative and Holistic Medicine

I also thank the many radiant ladies who have traveled this cancer journey and shared chapters of their stories with me. So many did not want to be mentioned by name, but wanted to pass along an insight or experience they'd had that might benefit another woman. To them, a heartfelt thank you.

Acknowledgements

A book comes together because of the support of so many people. To Donna Taft, Bill Overton, Jeff Reuter, and those others at AuthorHouse who contributed to this project, thank you for your support and work. To my family (Alan and Gerry Heckler, Karen Thompson and Jennifer Burran), who read and reread the manuscript during its various phases, offering wonderful insights and thoughts along the way, thank you. To Jane Garvin, who is without doubt one of the loveliest people I know and a cheerleader extraordinaire for this project, thank you.

By far, one of the biggest thank yous goes to my editor, Jeanne Wilson. We have a book because of the work that Jeanne did to turn my storytelling into words that matter. How disappointing it must have been for Jeanne, a teacher, that six months later she was still correcting the exact same grammatical errors for me. And, if it wasn't a grammatical error, it was thinning some of the generous supply of question marks and exclamation points. For you see, when I write, if I am making a point, I like to use at least three exclamation points. There for a while, Jeanne was hoping to find five at one time. But, no such luck Jeanne, until now. Thank you, thank you, thank you Jeanne for all you did. I hope that, should this book succeed in reaching, speaking to, and touching many people facing a cancer journey, that you know that its effectiveness will be in large part because of you!!!!!

About The Author

Donna Heckler is a global brand strategy executive, brand marketing thought leader, author, and speaker. Co-author of the book *The Truth About Creating Brands People Love*, she has influenced and led global brand marketing efforts for companies such as Energizer, Cardinal Health, Ingersoll-Rand, and others.

Ms. Heckler learned in August of 2010 that she had Stage 3, HER2 breast cancer just as she was beginning a new global marketing executive job. As she went through chemo, multiple surgeries, and radiation while tackling a new position, she kept a blog of her many cancer experiences.

Ms. Heckler is actively involved in her community and supports a number of organizations. She currently serves as the Chairperson of the Board for the Cancer Support Community of St. Louis. Ms. Heckler was named by the *St. Louis Business Journal* as one of the outstanding business leaders in St. Louis under the age of 40, and she frequently serves as a guest speaker on branding for various organizations and universities. Ms. Heckler has a B.A. in Zoology from DePauw University and an M.B.A. in Marketing from Indiana University.